CHILDREN'S MINISTRY LEADERSHIP

Recruiting and Training
Children's Ministry Leaders

DR. ANDREW T. KNIGHT

ISBN: 1500752053

ISBN 13: 9781500752057

DEDICATION

    This book was a result of the research and application of my major ministry project for the Doctor of Ministry. Though I have many to thank for their help along the way, I would be remiss if I did not thank Dr. Dell Johnson for his twenty-five year friendship. While in Bible College Dr. Johnson challenged his students to write books... so here you go! His zeal for biblical scholarship, the Textus Receptus, Christian education, and a love for children was contagious. Without his encouragement throughout my doctoral work this project might never had been completed. Thank you Dr. Johnson for your friendship!

TABLE OF CONTENTS

CHAPTER ONE

INTRODUCTION

Perception of the Problem

Trinity Baptist Church, an Independent Baptist church in Jacksonville, Florida has focused on increasing the enrollment and development of the children's ministry. For the ministry to have a lasting impact, it must reach [1] the impressionable and receptive minds of the community. George Barna, author of *Transforming Children into Spiritual Champions*, stated, "Why focus on this particular slice of the youth market? Because if you want to shape a person's life—whether you are most concerned about his or her moral, physical, intellectual, emotional or economic development—it is during these critical eight years that lifelong habits, values, beliefs and attitudes are formed." [2] According to Barna, these first years, sometimes referred to as the formative years, are fruitful in reaching children for the Lord. Based on Barna's research, young children are seemingly most receptive to the message of the gospel. Local churches are faced with the challenge

---

1 For the purpose of this paper, the definition of 'reach' will be: For a child to come to a saving knowledge of salvation through faith in Jesus Christ.

2 George Barna, *Transforming Children into Spiritual Champions* (Ventura: Regal Books, 2003), 18.

1

of attempting to impact their culture through recruiting and training workers in order to maintain a concentrated effort to reach children.

Thom Rainer, author of *Breakout Churches*, writes, "From 1990 to 2000 the U.S. population grew from 248 million to 281 million, a thirteen percent increase. In that same period, worship attendance in American churches grew by less than 1 percent."[3] Such a decline may indicate the local church needs to reach the children in its community. In addition, this decline may be attributed to a cultural shift. David Jeremiah exposes a cultural shift when he writes, "When the Bible was pervasive in culture, there was no skepticism about its truth or its relevance. But a slow, subtle, steady shift in how our nation views the Bible has pushed it out of the center of culture to the inconsequential edges. It has been marginalized beyond anything I could ever have imagined as a youth."[4] Perhaps this marginalization of the Bible has impacted children's ministries as well.

This study sought to recruit, train, and involve church members in the children's ministry at Trinity Baptist Church in Jacksonville, Florida. This was accomplished by developing recruitment and training strategies gleaned from churches with strong children's ministries.

Description of the Problem

Trinity Baptist Church has a children's ministry with two distinctly different but equally important areas of ministry. The two are divided terms of maintaining and gaining. The maintenance aspect of the children's ministry caters to children that are brought to church by their parents. This ministry is vital, but continues to have a constant labor shortage. Seventy-five volunteer positions are advertised in the weekly prayer bulletin but little improvement has been made. In the

---

3 Thom S. Rainer, *Breakout Churches* (Grand Rapids, MI: Zondervan, 2005), 73.

4 David Jeremiah, *I Never Thought I'd See the Day: Culture at the Crossroads* (New York, NY: Yates & Yates Publishers, 2011), 177.

outreach area, the bus ministry has been in decline for over two decades. This decline may either be intentional or a lack of commitment to the children's ministry.

The children's ministry has not been adequately recruiting and training workers to maintain and grow the children's ministry. The leadership appears to be incapable and ineffective. Each successive leader of the children's ministry has seen a decline of effectiveness in the children's outreach and overall children's program. The philosophy of the overall ministry has moved from one of developing servant-leaders to one that is developing a culture of entertainment and shallow Christianity. This shift may likely be what has hindered their ability to recruit servant leaders. The pulpit at Trinity Baptist Church has been silent with regard to recruiting and training workers for the children's ministry. Also, the current preaching and teaching has not appeared to be directly connected to any outreach associated with the children's ministry. There have been no direct applications between the preaching and the application to the children's ministry during the project period.

Trinity Baptist Church has a need for church members to be involved with the development of a children's ministry in order to reach future generations in their community. Gordon Lovik states:

> In order for the child to realize a right relationship with God, the parents as well as the child must understand parental responsibility as taught in Scripture. The exact teachings of Scripture must be understood as principles in order to achieve the proper training of the child. Since the only authoritative source is the Bible itself, it must be the authority regarding the goals in the education of the child. [5]

---

5 Gordon H. Lovik, "Christian Education," *Central Bible Quarterly* (Spring 1966): 6.

Daniel Whitehead, concerning the connection between the Great Commission and children's church, writes:

> Although the instruction of children is not new to this day and society, the development of the children's church approach is quite recent. For many years, the Sunday school has been accepted and utilized in the pursuance of the Great Commission in a graded manner to teach children, but little thought has been given to providing a preaching program on a graded scale. [6]

Although many people attend church, most are not engaged in the work of the Great Commission. It appears that most parents have only considered what a church can do for their child and don't necessarily reach out to children who are not their own.

Importance of the Problem

Barna's research regarding parental attitudes revealed the following, "When asked to identify the most significant or challenging issues facing their children under the age of 13... Challenges pertaining to their faith were mentioned by only 3% of parents." [7] Therefore, there are two areas that need to be addressed in the contemporary context of the local church.

First is the level of conviction parents possess regarding the transfer of faith to their children. Marcia Bunge discussed parents' lack of conviction regarding their children's involvement in Sunday school. Bunge stated, "Many parents do not know what their children are

---

6 Daniel C. Whitehead, "A Successful Children's Church Program," Central Bible Quarterly (Winter 1973): 4.

7 George Barna, "Survey Reveals Challenges Faced by Young People," The Barna Group, http://www.barna.org/family-kids-articles/96-survey-reveals-challenges-faced-by-young-people (accessed October 12, 2011).

learning in Sunday school, let alone participate in intergenerational or family religious education programs; and parents also are not given the sense that they are primarily responsible for the faith formation for children." [8] Many children follow patterns and assume the values of their parents. The local church that does not emphasize the significance of a children's ministry will not likely mentor parents in the area of a child's spiritual development.

The second issue concerns the priorities parents have with regard to their children. Based on an interview with parents, Barna revealed the following statistics, "The least significant issues to address were improving the spiritual state of the country (53%); increasing people's sense of belonging to a community (45%); enhancing the moral content within entertainment (44%); and advancing the health of Christian churches (44%)." [9] Barna's survey indicated the low priority parents have for their children's spiritual well-being. The local church has a responsibility to invest in a children's ministry as it endeavors to reach the next generation. John W. Kennedy stated, "For generations, ministry leaders have been proclaiming the importance of evangelizing children." [10] The need to reach children is an ongoing process from generation to generation. Kennedy continued, "Research compiled by his Barna Group shows that children between the ages of 5 and 13 have a 32 percent probability of accepting Jesus Christ as their Savior." [11] This research indicates the importance of reaching children at a young age.

---

8   Marcia J. Bunge, "Biblical and Theological Perspectives on Children, Parents, and 'Best Practices' for Faith Formation: Resources for Children, Youth, and Family Ministry Today," *A Journal of Theology* (Winter 2008): 349.

9   George Barna, "Americans are most Worried about Children's Future," The Barna Group, http://www.barna.org/family-kids-articles/97-americans-are-most-worried-about-childrens-future (accessed October 12, 2011).

10   John W. Kennedy, "The 4-14 Window: The Push on Child Evangelism Targets the Critical Early Years," Christianity Today (July 2004): 53.

11   Ibid.

Lynda Freeman states, "Anyone can provide a babysitting service for kids, but a children's ministry is much more than that. As you develop your purpose, keep in mind the purpose God has for parents (Deut. 6.1-9; Psalm 78.1-8). The church must not replace parents." [12] Based upon Freeman's statement, the local church has a responsibility to be involved with the spiritual development of children. However, parents are not relieved of their duty at home to teach Bible truths.

The Problem in Biblical Perspective

Recruiting and Training Children's Ministry Leaders

Jesus, regarding the priority of ministering to children, states, "Suffer little children, and forbid them not, to come unto me: for of such is the kingdom of heaven (Matt. 19.14)." A biblical priority for churches is to reach children and aid in their spiritual development. Barna comments, "The Bible makes it quite clear that children are uniquely special to God." [13] Children need to be taught biblical principles with the understanding that people are made in God's image. Genesis 1.27, "So God created man in his own image, in the image of God created he him; male and female created he them." Lawrence Richards writes about the importance of the children's ministry in the first century church, "But there is a most compelling reason to believe that members of the early church did draw their children into fellowship of local communities and did instruct them in the Word of God." [14] II Timothy 3.15 states, "And that from a child thou hast known the holy scriptures, which

---

12 Lynda Freeman, "Sizing Up Sunday School Curriculum: How to Find the Perfect Fit," *Your Church* (May/June 2008): 42.

13 Barna, *Transforming Children into Spiritual Champions*, 44.

14 Lawrence O. Richards, *Children's Ministry* (Grand Rapids, MI: Zondervan, 1983), 46.

are able to make thee wise unto salvation through faith which is in Christ Jesus." One can then see the long history that churches have had in passing the gospel down through children from one generation to the next.

Ronald Horton shared the importance of children's ministry in shaping the next generation of believers by saying, "Education—from the moment a child is born, certain forces are at work influencing his development." [15] The need for churches to develop a children's ministry is for salvation, as well as sanctification according to Larry D. Pettegrew who states, "An all-inclusive principle of children's work is to have a biblical goal. The goal of all children's work is to saturate the hearts and minds of children with the Word of God. This may seem too simple at first, but it is basic in making young disciples for Christ." [16]

William H. Willimon notes, "Thus, children become a kind of paradigm, a symbol for how one gets into this strange, counter-cultural kingdom. Here is a kingdom where the door is very small, to be entered only by those who know their poverty, their vulnerability, and their neediness." [17] D. Bruce Lockerbie gives a summary of the biblical mandate to teach children the Bible, "From the time that Moses received the Law of God, the people of Israel had known their responsibility to teach children." [18] This study will examine the need for a children's ministry as shown through scriptural evidence.

---

15 Ronald A. Horton, *Christian Education: Its Mandate and Mission* (Greenville: Bob Jones University Press, 1992), 3-4.

16 Larry D. Pettegrew, "Biblical Principles for Children's Work," *Central Bible Quarterly* (Fall 1967): 34.

17 William H. Willimon, "Preaching to Children," *Faith and Mission* (Fall 1985): 26.

18 D. Bruce Lockerbie, *A Passion for Learning: A History of Christian Thought on Education* (Colorado Springs, CO: Purposeful Design Publications, 2007), 3.

Old Testament

Deuteronomy 6.1-7

One of the foundations for children's ministry is found in Deuteronomy 6.1, "Now these *are* the commandments, the statutes, and the judgments, which the LORD your God commanded to teach you, that ye might do *them* in the land whither ye go to possess it." Moses commanded the Israelites to learn God's law. He then instructed the Israelites to teach their children. Deuteronomy 6.2 states, "That thou mightest fear the LORD thy God, to keep all his statutes and his commandments, which I command thee, thou, and thy son, and thy son's son, all the days of thy life; and that thy days may be prolonged." This teaching principle is evidenced by Moses' writings. This philosophy of transferring God's knowledge may be applied within the New Testament church.

Although, churches have a duty to partner with parents in maintaining a children's ministry, the greater responsibility belongs to the parents according to John Walvoord who states:

> God's people were responsible to meditate on these commands, to keep them in their hearts. This enabled them to understand the Law and to apply it correctly. Then the parents were in position to impress them on their children's hearts also. The moral and biblical education of the children was accomplished best not in a formal teaching period each day but when the parents, out of concern for their own lives as well as their children's, made God and His Word the natural topic of a conversation which might occur anywhere and anytime during the day. [19]

---

[19] John F. Walvoord, and Roy B. Zuck, *The Bible Knowledge Commentary: An Exposition of the Scriptures* (Wheaton IL: Victor Books, 1985), 274-275.

A child's religious education should be engrafted into family life as seen in Deuteronomy 6.7, "And thou shalt teach them diligently unto thy children, and shalt talk of them when thou sittest in thine house, and when thou walkest by the way, and when thou liest down, and when thou risest up."

Proverbs 22.6

The significance of a children's ministry was communicated by King Solomon when he wrote, "Train up a child in the way he should go: and when he is old, he will not depart from it (Prov. 22.6)." The teaching emphasis in this passage indicates the foresight to instruct children when they are young to ensure these truths would be with them as they grow into adults. Charles Bridges explained the significance of a children's ministry:

> Everything hangs on his training. Two lie before him—the way in which he would go, headlong to ruin; and the way in which he should go, the pathway to heaven. The rule for training implies obliquity. A young and healthy tree shoots straight upwards and instead of putting forth crooked and deformed branches, gives promise of a fine and fruitful maturity. [20]

Therefore, the evidence in Proverbs indicates the necessity of parents to involve their children in a children's ministry. In addition, Scripture indicates that an effective children's ministry will produce a favorable spiritual outcome for the children.

---

20 Charles Bridges, *A Commentary on Proverbs* (Carlisle: The Banner of Truth Trust, 1846), 402.

New Testament

Matthew 18.2-3

The importance of the children's ministry is evidenced by the words of Jesus when he states, "And Jesus called a little child unto him, and set him in the midst of them (Matt. 18.2)." Jesus, in His earthly ministry, exemplified spending time ministering and teaching children about Himself. He further states, "Verily I say unto you, except ye be converted, and become as little children, ye shall not enter into the kingdom of heaven (Matt. 18.3)." Adam Clarke, in his commentary on this passage in Matthew, shows Jesus equating the heart of a child to one of a spiritual person when he comments, "Unless ye be clothed with the spirit of humility, ye cannot enter into the spirit, design, and privileges of my spiritual and eternal kingdom." [21] Evidently, children's ministry is necessary as the hearts of children are readied to receive the message of the gospel. Clarke comments on the spiritual ripeness of children by saying, "Be as truly without worldly ambition, and the lust of power, as little children are, who act among themselves as if all were equal." [22] The significance of a children's ministry is seen as the hearts and minds of children are described as untainted from the world. Clarke explained that children have a sense of innocence enabling them to receive the things of God.

Mark 10.14-15

Mark recorded evidence of Jesus' heart for children and thus the priority of the church when he wrote, "But when Jesus saw

---

21 Adam Clarke, *Matthew to Acts,* vol. 5 of *Clarke's Commentary* (New York, NY: Abingdon Press, 1832), 182.
22 Ibid.

it, he was much displeased, and said unto them, Suffer the little children to come unto me, and forbid them not: for of such is the kingdom of God (Matt. 10.14)." Albert Barnes further developed this thought when he noted, "Saw the conduct of His disciples. *Was displeased.* Because it was a pleasure to Him to receive and bless the little children." [23] Evidence shows that Jesus loved and blessed the children, thus setting the example for churches to invest into a children's ministry.

Jesus dealt with the receptivity of a child's heart in Mark 10.15, "Verily I say unto you, whosoever shall not receive the kingdom of God as a little child, he shall not enter therein." Mark's record gives evidence of the priority and fruitfulness of a children's ministry. Barnes addressed the receptivity of children when he wrote, "With the temper and spirit of a child—teachability, mild, humble, and free from prejudice and obstinacy."[24] The message being relayed is that a person likely will be saved as a child. Thus, it is important to implement a children's ministry to reach the current generation.

Recruiting and Training Children's Ministry Leaders

One objective of the local church might be to encourage believers to reach the next generation for Christ. A children's ministry will accomplish this objective by building a Christian foundation in both the children's lives as well as the lives of the parents and other church workers. Scripture seems to support the idea that the optimum time one comes to faith in Christ is as a child.

---

23 Albert Barnes, *Barnes' Notes, The Gospels* (Grand Rapids, MI: Baker Book House, 1885), 367.

24 Ibid.

The Problem in Contemporary Thought

Regarding parenting, Barna states:

Parenting by default is what Barna termed 'the path of least resistance.' In this approach, parents do whatever comes naturally to the parent, as influenced by cultural norms and traditions. The objective is to keep everyone – parent, child, and others as happy as possible, without having the process of parenting dominate other important or personalized aspects of the parents' life. [25]

Based on Barna's assertion, churches have a cultural impact on the way parents think concerning the enrollment of children in Sunday school. The children's ministry is an aid to the parents, not a spiritual substitute. Daily, parents should be the primary spiritual coaches to their children. They have the ultimate responsibility for their children's spiritual welfare.

David Hegg describes the cultural problem with parents, children, and children's ministry when he states, "Today, we are seeing the balance between Sunday school and church erode. What was always meant to be taken together has today become optional. Many people attend one or the other and never realize that they are depriving themselves of a necessary component of Christian living." [26] Involving children in a children's ministry should not be optional in order for them to develop spiritually.

John and Judy Allison discuss the parent's responsibility be involved in their children's spiritual development by not only placing their child into a children's ministry, but also being involved in the

---

25 George Barna, "Research Shows Parenting Approach Determines whether Children become Devoted Christians," *The Barna Group* (2009): 2.

26 David W. Hegg, "Children and Congregational Worship: When, Why, and How?" *Reformation and Revival* (Winter 2001): 109.

ministry themselves. The Allisons deal with the problem of parents subjugating the responsibility of their children to the local church when they state:

> A problem that has been observed in Christianity today is that many parents rely on the church to teach their children. Taking a child to Sunday school every Sunday is an excellent practice, but it should not take the place of instruction at home. The parent is the adult that will make the deepest impression upon a child. [27]

Based on this insight, parents should be engaged in their children's spiritual development, as well as their own. Parents cannot raise spiritually mature children by proxy. Parents, as the Allisons explained, are the only ones that can be the continual spiritual coaches to their children.

Edward Hayes discussed specialized ministries, such as children's ministries, to describe how ministries have become more focused. Hayes states, "Today, child evangelism efforts are marked by increasing institutionalization and agency expansion. Specialization has entered the Christian marketplace, and organizations abound. Reaction and counteraction call for sound formulations and standards for proper assessment of their worth." [28]

Though there may be multiple directions a local church can take, it is important for a church to invest in a children's ministry. This study will endeavor to document the practices of four children's ministries that have involved both children and parents.

---

27 John P. Allison, and Judy V. Allison, "Parenting as Discipleship," *Ashland Theological Journal* (1997): 53.
28 Edward L. Hayes, "Evangelism of Children," *Bibliotheca Sacra* (July 1975): 251.

Summary of the Project

Description of the Project

The recruiting and training was extended from the biblical context to the current cultural trends. The sources of this research have included reference works, books, theological journals and articles, dissertations, and internet sources. This project began with the project director interviewing three pastors in New England churches. After transferring to Jacksonville, FL, the interviews continued with the children's pastor at Trinity Baptist Church, and the principal of the elementary department at Trinity Christian Academy. Training Bible studies were prepared and taught for the purpose of recruiting and equipping leaders for the children's ministry. Two couples were surveyed before and after the training classes.

The Rationale

The rationale was to develop a children's ministry training program for workers to impact and reach future generations. The results of this research will help the leadership focus on reaching children and training parents to become leaders in the children's ministry at Trinity Baptist Church in Jacksonville, Florida.

The Goals

The projected outcome was to recruit and develop more leaders for the children's ministry. More children have been enrolled into the children's ministry as leaders are trained. These trained leaders, in turn, recruit others to enroll more children into the children's ministry.

The Strategies and Setting

This research was conducted in part from conducting interviews with three New England pastors of Independent Baptist churches, one pastor in Jacksonville, Florida, and one interview with the elementary school principal at Trinity Christian Academy in Jacksonville, Florida.

The project began in New England and then moved to a new ministry and setting in Jacksonville, Florida. While at a previous church planting ministry on the North Shore of Boston, the project director was in a house fire and was 80% burned to the third and fourth degree. During the time of the major ministry project, his doctor strongly recommended that he move out of the cold climate. The transition to a warm, humid climate has been necessary for long-term health.

These churches and the Christian school all have a long history with the enrollment and development of their children's ministries. The data produced from this research was gathered by the project director. The participants of these interviews were asked to provide any record keeping data from their respective children's ministries. This data was to include enrollment strategies, attendance of the children's ministry, overall church and school attendance, ministry job descriptions, and the back ground check process of the children's workers. The final data aspects were collected though surveys as a result of working with the bus captains in the bus ministry, and leading the community Bible classes where training was conducted.

The settings where the interviews were conducted in New England and Jacksonville, Florida were two vastly different subcultures. George Barna demonstrated the differences through his research on the cities that are "The Most Post-Christian Cities in America." [29] Barna's research showed Boston, Massachusetts ranked

---

29 George Barna, "Wherever My Mind Takes Me, America's Most Secular Cities," Sarvodaya, http://romneymanassa.wordpress.com/2013/04/16/americas-most-secular-and-religious-cities/ (accessed September 9, 2013).

seventh and Hartford, Connecticut ranked fifth in terms of the most secular cities in the country. Meanwhile, according to Barna's research Jacksonville, Florida ranked 20th in terms of "America's Most Bible-Minded Cities." [30] The difference in the percentage of the populous that are more secular minded versus the percentages of the populous that are more Bible-minded change the difference in the level of church attendance and number of children in children's ministry drastically.

In the interviewed New England churches, the average attendance ranged from 100-600. These Independent Baptist churches are rare. In addition to the distance between Baptist churches, the population density is a factor in regard to church attendance. Because the New England churches are so much smaller, a majority of the church's only paid staff people are the pastor and maybe a part-time secretary. Many times all the music and the youth leaders were entirely volunteer based. When New Englanders are approached with the gospel there is a large sense of indifference, but those that do get saved tend to take it seriously. The predominant religion in New England is Catholicism. The culture that surrounds the Baptist churches in New England has a view of biblical Christianity that is highly influenced by Catholicism. The population in New England is fairly stayed. That is to say that generation after generation will live and die within a 20 mile radius. This has an effect on churches as the mindset is one of consistency, even in regard to religion.

Trinity Baptist Church is almost 100 years old and had an average attendance of 2,200 people that attend weekly between the three weekend services. It has eight paid pastors plus support staff. This does not include the paid staff at the three rescue missions, the Bible college, and the Christian school. With regard to the subculture in Jacksonville, it is not true to say that everyone has heard the gospel, but Christianity is pervasive within the sub-culture. The other sub-culture difference is seen in the application of ministry as Jacksonville is

---

30 Ibid.

a transient town. There are five military installations in Jacksonville, and it is a port city that has a large trade presence.

The Assumptions

The project director has made several assumptions about the research of the children's ministry. Children's ministries beginning in the 1970s and in the South are two different cultures with different outcomes. With the advent of the internet, children will be more aware of their surroundings, but have a shortened attention span. Children and the overall culture may have a loss of innocence. Finally, the children's workers have been held to a higher screening standard in order to protect the children.

Demographics of the Project

The research portion of this project part has taken place at three churches; the first was at Meriden Hills Baptist Church in Meriden, Connecticut. This church was located in New Haven County. The current pastor has been innovative in outreach to children both in the Sunday school program and in the Christian school. The second church analyzed was Twin City Baptist Temple, located in Lunenburg, Massachusetts. This church was founded in 1974, and the current pastor is the founding pastor. The ministry includes a Christian day school, day care center, and a Christian radio station. The third church analyzed was Colonial Hills Baptist Church in Danbury, Connecticut, located in Fairfield County. This church was on the New York border and had a Christian day school. The founding pastor was interviewed to obtain data about Colonial Hills Baptist Church.

The city of Jacksonville, Florida has a population of approximately 836,000. The religious makeup of Jacksonville, Florida, ranked by George Barna, as "being 24% post-Christian in its

17

worldview." [31] The remaining 76% of the city was considered Christian in their worldview, but it also may be an overstatement to say that the cities' spiritual population is any deeper than the broadest sense of Christendom.

Trinity Baptist Church is the location and the children's ministry was the focus of the research project. The objective of the research was to develop a strategy for recruiting and training more children's ministry workers. The church had a well-established children's ministry but anticipates that it will be enhanced as the findings of this research project are applied. During the 40 years that the former pastor was there the church had a much larger membership and a large Christian school with over 1,500 students. As a result of these two aspects, the church had multi-generations within the congregation. Many of the staff were long-term employees of the ministry, and graduated from Trinity Baptist College. Jacksonville is a military town with many on active duty, but often these people do not become members of the church unless they stay in Jacksonville as civilians.

The Project Director

The project director was a church planter and most recently had done an internship at Trinity Baptist Church while applying the major ministry project. He has a desire to see children come to faith in Christ and watch them grow physically and spiritually. Through the implementation of this project, the goal is to see a children's ministry advanced and more children influenced for Christ.

---

31   George Barna, "Wherever My Mind Takes Me, America's Most Secular Cities," Sarvodaya, http://romneymanassa.wordpress.com/2013/04/16/americas-most-secular-and-religious-cities/ (accessed September 9, 2013).

The Project Participants

The first participants were the four pastors with established children's ministries. The four participating pastors are Ervan Burke, Twin City Baptist Temple; Chris Atkinson, Meriden Hills Baptist Church; Bob Critchton, Colonial Hills Baptist Church; and Paul Scott, Trinity Baptist Church.

The next group of participants included the children workers, bus captains, and other interested church members. Bus captains and children's workers attended the community Bible class. Bus captains and Sunday school workers recruited other children and promoted the program.

CHAPTER TWO

PROJECT RESEARCH AND DEVELOPMENT

Justification of the Project

Pastor Interviews

Interviews were conducted with four pastors who have been involved with children's ministries. These pastors were asked a series of questions regarding their strategies of training children's workers and enrolling children into their respective ministries. The results from these interviews were analyzed for strengths, weaknesses, and similarities.

The context of the project changed when the project director moved the setting of the project from a New England church plant to a large southern church in Jacksonville, Florida. Much of the data collected from the New England pastors was applicable to the large church setting in the South. The process of recruiting and training leaders for the children's ministry was much the same in both locations. The major differences were the amount of staff and other resources that the large, Southern church had that the New England churches did not. The information applied in the major ministry project dealt the resourcefulness of Pastor Bob Critchon when he turned his public school bus route into a teaching time of Bible verses and songs while he drove them to school. Resourcefulness was required in finding opportunities where the church would allow the major ministry project to be applied.

The data derived from Pastor Erven Burke's interview was used by applying his ability to organize and motivate people to reach others with the gospel. The interview with Pastor Chris Atkenson highlighted his ability to focus on reaching and ministering to children. Pastor Atkenson provided inspiration.

The strategies for children's ministry enrollment were presented to the community Bible class. A series of lessons was employed to present the need, the methods, and the desired results to be accomplished in the Trinity Baptist Church children's ministry. The Bible lessons were used to enlist leaders to serve in the outreach and development of the children's ministry.

Project Research

The research data gathered from academic sources as well as interviews with four pastors helped the project director assimilate the strategy for a children's ministry. Three problems within the scope of the children's ministry were addressed. First, was Trinity Baptist Church effectively enrolling children into their children's ministry? Second, was there effective and ongoing training to develop leaders for the children's ministry? Third, was there a plan to recruit parents to be become leaders in the children's ministry?

Concerning the issue of parents who have little conviction regarding the spiritual transformation of their children, Marva Dawn addresses the problem by asserting, "Parents need the total support of the entire Christian community, of a vital body of believers who contribute to the passing on of the faith ... parents are not equipped for their critical role in the shaping of character in their children..." [32]

Nancy DeMoss, author of *Lies Women Believe: And the Truth that Sets them Free,* deals with the lies some women tell themselves when their children are not living in a Christian manner. DeMoss states, "The first [lie] is that they have no control or influence over how their children have turned out—that they are not responsible, that the situation could not be helped. Believing this lie leads parents to throw off personal responsibility and to feel that they are helpless victims." [33] Perhaps this is one reason parents do not have a conviction regarding the spiritual transformation of their children.

Ivy Beckwith argued for the importance of parents having a conviction regarding the spiritual transformation of their children. Beckwith states:

> ...family is the most important arena for a child's spiritual development and soul care. Even families who never attend church nor consider issues of spirituality and ethics in their decision-making are spiritually forming their children. They are teaching their children that these things don't matter in the same way that families who do seek out lives of faith teach their children that these things do matter. [34]

It appears that parents either teach their children to live godly, or by default, ungodly lives in every circumstance. As Pastor Critchton indicated in his interview, parents should not be flippant concerning

---

32   Marva J. Dawn, *Is it a Lost Cause: Having the Heart of God for the Church's Children* (Grand Rapids, MI: William B. Eerdmans Publishing Company, 1997), 104-105.

33   Nancy Leigh DeMoss, *Lies Women Believe: And the Truth that Sets them Free* (Chicago, IL: Moody Publishers, 2001), 183.

34   Ivy Beckwith, *Postmodern Children's Ministry: Ministry to Children in the 21st Century* (Grand Rapids, MI: Zondervan, 2004), 102.

their children's spiritual condition. "Teach the parents that the child is on loan from God, and that the child has an eternal soul that may go to hell. Ask the parents, 'How would you feel if your child went to hell?' Ask the parent, 'How would you feel if your child went to prison?' Then make the connection to eternal punishment."[35]

In reference to the view held by parents concerning their children's spiritual development as a low priority, Christenson describes a principle of leading children by example, "Parents who want their children to know God must cultivate their own relationship with God. First and foremost this means a life of prayer. No amount of moral instruction, firm discipline, religious instruction, or church going can make up for the lack of a praying parent." [36] Children learn by watching their parents. Furthermore, Christenson indicated that children learn more from their parent's example then by being in a formal class setting.

Erven Burke's interview yielded valuable information regarding the encouragement of parents to make spiritual development of their children a high priority. Burke stated, "Talk to the parents about their spiritual and devotional life. If parents don't have it, the children won't either." [37]

Michael Anthony, author of *Perspectives on the Children's Spiritual Formation: 4 Views*, discussed Mark 9.33-37 in which Jesus gave an example as to why children's ministry is so important. The biblical context applies to adults who have an interest in the spiritual development of children. Anthony states, "Through His actions and Words, Jesus reveals the value He holds for the child as a significant part of the faith community. So precious to God is the child that He uses this little one to teach the disciples by simply placing this child

---

35　See Appendix C.

36　Larry Christenson, *The Christian Family* (Minneapolis, MN: Bethany Fellowship, 1970), 159.

37　See Appendix B.

before them." [38] Anthony pointed to Jesus' earthly ministry for parents to consider the importance of children's spiritual development. This biblical account serves as a precedent for local churches to follow.

Often, the budget allotted to the children's ministry is inadequate and disproportionate to the overall church budget. Michael Anthony dealt with this issue from the perspective of growing churches. He states, "More and more churches are realizing that a major factor in church growth is a well-staffed and trained children's ministry team. The most effective ministry models have professionals leading the team due to the heavy demands of programmatic designs." [39] As a result of this trend more churches are hiring professionally trained leaders and more funds are required to operate the various church ministries, including the children's ministry. Pastor Atkenson, regarding the percentage of the church budget allocated to the children's ministry, responded, "Five percent for the children and youth combined. Including the Christian school it is thirty percent of the church's budget is allocated to children's ministries." [40] This church has an attendance of about 100 people. Pastor Bob Critchton appropriated much more of the church budget to the children's ministry. When asked about his children's ministry budget Critchton answered, "Twenty-five percent of the church budget went to the children's ministry." [41] This church attendance grew to about 600 people.

There are three reasons why local churches should increase their human resources and budgets in order to reach children for the Lord. Reaching children is not just about church growth but rather it is strategically positioning the local churches to accomplish their part of the Great Commission. Biblical evidence for reaching children will be

---

38 Michael Anthony, *Perspectives on the Children's Spiritual Formation: 4 Views* (Nashville, TN: B & H Academic, 2006), 51.

39 Ibid., 1.

40 See Appendix A.

41 See Appendix C.

documented, as well as if they are not reached during childhood they may not be reached at all.

Reason 1: The next generation may be won or lost in the classroom. Don Closson understands this battle, when he states, "Relativism, the view that truth and absolute values do not exist, is the governing mechanism by which people solve moral dilemmas in our institutions of higher learning." [42] According to Closson, a secular author, the most influential time is during a child's school years. This is all the more true with regard to the gospel.

Reason 2: The population growth is a factor when considering the work of the Great Commission through the children's ministry. The World Population Review reported, "The most recent estimate was carried out in 2012 by the United States Census Bureau and it was estimated that the state's population had reached 19,317,568." [43] The Report continued, "If growth continues at roughly the same rate, by the time that the next Census is undertaken in 2020, numbers should have comfortably burst through 20 million, and probably even past 21 million." [44] The population growth serves as a measurement, in relationship to the conversion rate, of how and if churches are keeping up with the growing population.

Reason 3: The most fruitful group of people to minister to are children. Elmer Towns was convinced of this fact when he wrote, "Kids this young will formulate their ideas about Jesus, the church and the future. If you influence them as children, your ministry continues as they become youth and adults … you influence them for life." [45] Towns points out the spiritual benefit of reaching children early and

---

42 Don Closson, *Kids, Classrooms, & Contemporary Education* (Grand Rapids, MI: Kregel Publications, 2000), 98.

43 Author Unknown, "Population of Florida 2013," World Population Review, http://worldpopulationreview.com/united-states/florida (accessed October 12, 2013).

44 Ibid.

45 Elmer L. Towns, *10 Sunday Schools that Dared to Change* (Ventura: Regal Books, 1993), 45.

how it is sure to impact children for the remainder of their lives. This point is confirmed by John 15.8, "Herein is my Father glorified, that ye bear much fruit; so shall ye be my disciples." A fruitful ministry is one that is reaching children.

Similar Projects

Jon Lyle Whatley discussed the importance of the children's ministry by arguing, "The worker in children's evangelism must not forget that Christianity is always just one generation from extinction." [46] Whatley continued by discussing the need for a separate church service for children apart from the adult worship service. However, he did not present the other side of the argument. He neglected the benefits of children being in close proximity to their parents, and also the benefits of the influence parents have concerning godliness and worship.

Harold Twigg explained the need for enrolling children into a children's ministry by age group due to the changing family dynamic. He states, "A good indication of adequate need can be quickly ascertained by tabulating the number of pupils enrolled in the Sunday school within the age group being considered to become part of the children's church." [47] Twigg did not discuss the importance of the parents' example in worship for children.

Mark Seymour dealt with the administration of the children's ministry. He focused on the successful aspects of the children's ministry. He explains, "There are several things which help to make the program successful. The quality of the program itself, the way in which it is presented, the right leadership, the needs which the program meets;

---

46 Jon Lyle Whatley, "So now You've got a Children's Church" (Doctor of Ministry Dissertation, Luther Rice University, 1982), 3.
47 Harold Byron Twigg, "Train Up a Child – A Children's Church Manual" (Doctor of Ministry Dissertation, Luther Rice University, 1982), 5.

all of these things affect the success or failure of the program." [48] Seymour addressed the procedures and policies of the children's program, including the creation of a manual for the execution of children's ministry programs.

Project Content and Design

The project director investigated four churches regarding to their children's ministries, and the recruitment, assimilation, and retention of the children's workers. He observed the children's ministry at Trinity Baptist Church, and provided training to the children's workers.

A series of Bible lessons was developed focusing on how children's ministry relates to the Great Commission. Before and after the project, several weeks were spent visiting with bus captains and observing different areas of the children's ministry. A second survey was given to the participants to measure their growth and level of commitment.

The measurement of this growth was not based on the number of children enrolled in the children's ministry but rather the progress that was made training leaders to enroll more children into the ministry. Each one of the participants completed the survey gauging the progress of their understanding of biblical leadership. This major ministry project was applied and observed in the children's ministry at Trinity Baptist Church in Jacksonville, Florida.

---

48 Mark Benson Seymour, "A Guide to Children's Ministry" (Doctor of Ministry Dissertation, Luther Rice University, 1988), 19.

CHAPTER THREE

PROJECT IMPLEMENTATION AND RECORDING

Project Preparation

The project was begun with the intention of implementing it in the context of a New England church plant. Two years after the Letter of Intent was written, the project director moved to Jacksonville, Florida and was a volunteer in a large, southern church instead of the pastor of a church plant in Connecticut.

Before the project director moved from the New England church plant setting he got a verbal commitment from the pastor at Trinity Baptist Church in Jacksonville, Florida to apply his major ministry project at their children's ministry. That objective was confirmed and committed to by the senior pastor. The move to Jacksonville was made, and membership was accepted at Trinity Baptist Church.

The project director was referred to the children's pastor, and was told that he would not be allowed to be involved in the children's ministry for one year. The children's pastor stated that, "he was the gate keeper of the children's ministry." The project director discussed this with the senior pastor, leading to a lunch meeting two weeks later with both pastors. The meeting was to find common ground for the project to be written and fit into the overall children's program. It was suggested that the project director help the children's pastor lead a parenting discussion class with parents at a public school as part of the project. The parent discussion class was scheduled twice and had full support of the principal. Although the class was planned for and supported by the leadership, the class failed. The children's pastor scheduled and promoted the parenting class in the middle of the work day. Not a single parent ever came. The class was canceled and the children's pastor or senior pastor never made any availability for the project director to work directly with the children's ministry at the church.

As a result, the focus of the project shifted away from actually enrolling children into the children's program to recruiting and training others to enroll children into the children's ministry. Though the project director was disappointed, when dealing in the ministry one must look at these matters as divine redirections from the Lord. The project director then offered to teach a new class focused on recruiting and training people as children's workers. A staff pastor agreed to the plan to apply the major ministry project to their stated need for more small groups to be started. The staff pastor also committed to send people that were not connected in a small group to the new group. Although the staff pastor never followed through, the project director was able to recruit new people to the training class. This class then served as the application for the project.

Implementation of the major ministry project began at Trinity Baptist Church by investigating all areas of the children's ministry. Two appointment meetings with the children's pastor at the church yielded a historical and a current perspective of the children's ministry. The meetings also served as an opportunity for problem solving and a search for common ground to work together.

In addition to meeting with church staff, the project director interviewed the elementary principle and toured the Christian school, including meeting all the teachers. This interview was productive as it revealed how the principal and teachers tied the

Christian school ministry to the local church ministry. The findings of this interview demonstrated a highly competent and motivated group that focused on academics and the salvation of the students and parents.

During the first visit to the small classroom where the monthly bus meeting was held, it was immediately apparent why the bus ministry was failing. There was no leadership, no vision, no motivation, and no inspiration to recruit and train more children's workers. The purpose of the observation was to find solutions that would make recruitment and training more effective.

The project director went out on bus visitation with three of the six bus captains. The purpose was to give instruction where needed. One bus captain couple had not been trained to instruct children and parents on why or how to follow the Lord in believer's baptism. This was a good opportunity for them to learn by observation. The time spent with the bus captains was also an opportunity to be of encouragement to the leaders.

The project director attended a meeting for the Sunday school staff pastors addressing leaders interested in leading a Sunday school class or a home Bible study. The director's objective was to use the Bible study to recruit and train more leaders for the children's ministry. The following week the project director met with one of the Sunday school staff pastors to confirm that this would be an acceptable venue for this Bible study group. This was agreed to by the staff pastor, though there was no follow through on his commitment to feed people into the group. The stated strategy was to connect many of the unconnected members in the 2,200 member church to small groups.

Weekly Bible studies were held to train and recruit more leaders for the children's ministry. The lesson plans were designed to prepare leaders in the basics so they would have the confidence to reach more children and families and recruit more leaders for training.

Project Data

The community class was launched to train more workers to enroll children. Spiritual growth in the Bible study group was evaluated by taking an inventory survey about enrolling children based upon biblical understanding and convictions of personal commitment. After the seventh Bible study, each attendee was given a second survey which gauged how ones biblical knowledge, understanding and commitment has changed or progresses in enrolling children into the children's ministry.

Community Class

Pre-training surveys were given to two couples that attend the Community Class. The surveys focused on the couple's present understanding of the gospel, the Great Commission, daily devotional life, spiritual gifts, and leadership abilities. This assessment will help the project director determine the participant's willingness to be placed or advanced in the children's ministry.

The post-training survey was given to two couples that attended the Bible study. This survey has shown the development of the children's workers commitment to the Great Commission, their convictions, blessings received, spiritual growth, and applied leadership in the children's ministry. These surveys helped the program director gain a better understanding of the participant's level of spiritual commitment in their personal lives and to the Great Commission.

Pre-Training Survey Results

The results of the pre-training survey revealed that both couples had a sound understanding of the gospel. Furthermore, responses with regard to the gospel were biblical and referenced repentance, whosoever salvation, and a child's age of accountability. The participants demonstrated their ability to give a clear, biblical presentation of the gospel to children.

The pre-training survey bore favorable results of the basic understanding and ability to communicate aspects of the Great Commission necessary to the children's ministry. Both couples understood that the Great Commission is directed at every believer, and understanding their responsibility. The participants also understood the inclusiveness of salvation, baptism, and Christian education within the Great Commission. From those that responded to the pre-training survey both couples also demonstrated the urgency in reaching children for the Lord and enrolling them in the Sunday school program by their understanding of the eminent return of Christ. The motivation to serve the Lord in the children's ministry was identified by their desire to be used by God.

The devotional lives of the children's workers have been uniformly consistent from both couples that participated in the survey. Their devotional lives consisted of Bible reading and prayer with other family members. The children's workers all expressed a desire for private devotion and public worship.

Both couples surveyed saw themselves as bus ministry leaders. They generally see the need for leader development in order for spiritual growth. They also see leadership opportunities as a gift and stewardship they are responsible to develop and apply. Most see their spiritual gift as a teacher and prophet, but more importantly as servants.

The pre-training surveys revealed that both couples were highly committed to reaching children for the Lord and enrolling them into the children's ministry. Both couples are at a high level of commitment in their private devotional lives and public ministry. They welcome growth, and if challenged to reach a higher level of spiritual and ministry development they would likely rise to the occasion.

Post-Training Survey Results

The post-training survey revealed a deep understanding of reaching children for the Lord. Those surveyed understood the importance of consistently keeping the Word of God before the children. The two couples sharing the gospel saw their own lives changed as well as the lives of those that received the gospel. The survey revealed a commitment to witnessing that extended beyond children's ministry, and to every area of their lives. Both couples understood that the Great Commission applied to them. They all practiced Scripture memory and saw the benefits of Scripture application in children's ministry.

Those surveyed and currently working in children's ministry, see the need to reach children early in life, believing there is a greater likelihood for salvation. They also all felt the influence of others and knew their example influenced those watching to be leaders in the children's ministry as well. Half of those surveyed had raised children in their home and had seen the benefit of having long-term spiritual influence on their children. All that took the survey acknowledged that Scripture memory was useful while witnessing to parents and children, as well as explaining baptism to new converts. One of the couples surveyed understood the importance of teaching eternal security as soon as possible after a child makes a profession of faith. All those surveyed understood the importance of baptism shortly following a child's conversion. One of those surveyed was prepared to make a baptism presentation to a child or parent.

All surveyed were convinced that reaching this generation for Christ will influence the next generation of children. They also understood the importance of influencing others for Christ as well as the godly individuals who have influenced them to be leaders in the children's ministry. Also, 50% understood the significance of how the children's ministry related to the local church, while 100% of the respondents understood that the children's ministry was an opportunity to exercise their God-given talents and abilities. They also believe the children's ministry was a stewardship, including their time, talent, and resources.

While the pre-training survey concentrated on revealing a general understanding of the children's ministry, such as the gospel, the Great Commission, devotions, leadership, and spiritual gifts, the post-training survey took a little different approach. The pre-training survey demonstrated a strong comprehension of biblical concepts necessary to working in the children's ministry. There was room for further development and not all were equally qualified.

The results from both the pre-training survey and the post-training survey demonstrated room for spiritual and leadership development. The post-training survey moved more toward a more specific understanding of the children's ministry. It also considered the Great Commission responsibilities, kingdom priorities, making presentations, teaching methods, leadership, and stewardship.

The pre-training survey looked deeper into the mentioned topics with regard to preparing leaders to reach children for the Lord. It did not consider as much application to the children's ministry as did the post-training survey. The post-training survey produced more complete outcomes since the questions were directed more toward children's ministry applications. In both the pre-training and post-training surveys, the participants all expressed a high level of commitment to the children's ministry. While working in the field with the participants, the project director found areas that needed further development, such as believer-baptism presentations. While some workers seemed comfortable with presenting salvation and believers-baptism there were other areas of development needed such as recruitment of workers and efficiencies in the Sunday school enrollment process. Since the project director was new to this church and the children's ministries, it allowed for a fresh look and the ability to make some contributions to the ministry's development and advancement. Some observations include ongoing development and leadership training, more aggressive recruitment of children's workers, more efficient Sunday school enrollment procedures, and a more concentrated approach to reaching the families and friends of the children already enrolled in the children's ministry.

Project Analysis

The project was unable to be fully implemented in the children's ministry at Trinity Baptist Church. The first challenge was for the project director, after moving to a new area, to find a church that would allow him to begin working in a church with the children to fulfill the project requirements. He did obtain a commitment from the senior pastor at Trinity Baptist Church. However, implementation of the project was difficult. The children's pastor told the project director he would not allow him to work in the children's ministry for one year. The project director had two meetings with the senior and children's pastor to find an acceptable way to implement his project while helping the ministry. The children's pastor committed to letting the project be applied while in the meetings, but in practice the project was not allowed to be fully implemented. The emphasis was then moved from enrolling children to training leaders to enroll children into the children's ministry. The project became an exercise of leadership.

The nature of the first survey dealt with the biblical understanding of the gospel. The biblical comprehension of the gospel and answers reported by both surveyed couples revealed a good understanding of the gospel. The aspects of acting by faith for salvation, repentance of sins, and urgency to share the gospel with children were affirmed by both surveyed couples.

The second survey dealt with the practice of the gospel's biblical knowledge and was measured favorably based on the participant's answers. The children's workers could only answer by their experience in the children's ministry. The two couples surveyed agreed that their job was to share the gospel with children.

In the pre-training, both couples understood the Great Commission, and included the need for Christian education. The personal requirements involved with the Great Commission were also to children's ministry. The response in the post-training survey revealed that being a soul-winner would affect those around them positively.

Three out of four were favorable in the pre-training survey with regard to devotional life and growth. When asked about memorizing the Word of God in the post-training survey, both couples responded positively. The higher response rate was due to Scripture memory already being used in the children's ministry presentations.

The pre-training survey revealed the couple's views on their children's ministry leadership. The results from the post-training survey found that both couples were not only leaders in the children's ministry but exercised that leadership to reach the children and also their fathers for the Lord. The emphasis on fathers came from a desire for parents to disciple their children.

Finally, the pre-training survey focused on spiritual gifts. Both couples believe they have a spiritual gift and the connection was made to the local church. The post-training survey revealed that both couples felt their service in the children's ministry was a stewardship of talents.

After careful analysis of the time the project director had spent with the children's workers in the field, in Bible study groups, and giving surveys, the results showed spiritual growth. The areas where growth was obvious were through biblical training, children's ministry, and leadership development.

Project Evaluation

The major ministry project began in New England with the intent to apply the project to a new church plant in South Windsor, Connecticut. The Letter of Intent was written while in Connecticut. Three New England senior pastors were chosen to be interviewed concerning the most effective ways to enroll children into the ministry. These three Baptist churches in New England all had Christian schools and were inclusive in the questions of their overall children's ministry. These interviews were informative and gave a good 40 year perspective of ministry.

Because of the health condition of the project director the church plant in South Windsor, Connecticut was forced to close. The project director's doctor told him to move south as a result of being burned over 80% of his body in a house fire. The project director had a pastor friend in Jacksonville, Florida and called on him for a new place to apply the major ministry project. This was the children's ministry at Trinity Baptist Church.

Upon relocating to Jacksonville, Florida the project director was introduced to the children's pastor. Several phone calls and meetings took place in order to understand the pastor's philosophy and vision. During the first few weeks in Jacksonville, two more meetings took place as part of the major ministry project. These interviews were held in the church office for the purpose of gathering information on the church's history and children's ministry, but also to brainstorm how to make the children's ministry more effective.

This church and children's ministry has undergone major changes in size, philosophy, and methods of outreach. Under the previous, long-term pastor the church was considered a fundamental Baptist church. The church held to the great hymns of the faith, exclusively used the King James Bible, and held standards of separation. The women and girls were dressed modestly, and the men and boys wore suites and ties. Under the previous pastor, the church attendance had swelled to over 4,000 people in weekly attendance. The Bible College was larger and all the students were required to work on the bus ministry every week. The church ran 66 buses all over the city picking up children for Sunday school.

At the present time, the current pastor has been there for 21 years. The church's philosophy under the current pastor has changed from being fundamental to contemporary. The Bible college students are no longer required to work on a bus route or in the children's ministry. The church used to hold weekly bus ministry training meetings on Wednesday nights, but currently, the bus training meetings are held once per month. The church now runs six buses into the community. The church's attendance is currently about 2,200 people. The children's ministry sees about 280 in weekly attendance with an enrollment of almost 600 children.

This past fall, the project director attended three of the monthly Wednesday night bus meetings held on the church campus with 10-12 people in attendance. He also visited the different bus routes with the bus captains. The bus captains all needed encouragement and assured that their service had value and was appreciated. This sense of demoralization was due to limited support and no weekly bus ministry meeting.

One bus captain couple allowed the project director to visit with the families of children who were seeking baptism after recently being saved. After several home visits and believers-baptism presentations, he sat down with the couple to discuss leading children in taking the step of baptism. Even though this couple had been serving for a number of years, they were never trained in educating families on believers-baptism. A lesson plan was added that addressed talking to the families about baptism. It also taught how to use the baptism visit as a soul-winning visit for those who may still need Christ.

After visiting with another bus captain, one that was more knowledgeable and had a Bible college education, the project director found concerns with the bus ministry efficiency. The bus captain was instructed to begin calling ahead and setting appointments with the parents so they would be available and his time was better spent. As a result of the project director's time in the field, the different bus captains were encouraged, given instruction, and became more confident and efficient.

The church announced they were in need of leaders to begin new community groups. The project director attended the community class informational meeting and it proved to be an opening for him to train children's ministry workers. After meeting with one of the staff pastors, arrangements were made to begin the training class with approved Bible lessons.

The project director interviewed the elementary school principal at Trinity Christian Academy. It was a great encouragement to see how this godly lady used her office to win many parents to Christ. It is no coincidence that her teachers were all soul-winners. It was reported the staff would make home and hospital visits, attend funeral services of anyone even remotely related to the school, or whatever else it took to win children and parents to Christ. The principal and her staff would hold open houses, invite parents and children to regular and special services, as well as invite the children to AWANA on Wednesday nights. The philosophy of this Christian school was to aggressively enroll children into the children's ministries while mentoring the parents to raise godly children.

CHAPTER FOUR

CONCLUSION

Knowledge Gained from Project

During the course of the research, Letter of Intent, and the application phase of the major ministry project, the project director learned a plethora of different methods to enroll children into children's ministry. The two methods used at Trinity Baptist Church and school are the bus ministry and the open enrollment of the Christian school. The method being added was the training of more leaders to enroll children into the children's ministry. It should be noted that the Sunday school and the Christian academy are both included when referring to the children's ministry.

Pastor Chris Atkenson and his wife demonstrate creativity as they seek to reach children for the Lord and their Christian school. Soon after Pastor Atkenson had taken the pastorate of this church, he decided to open a Christian school for the church children as well as the community children. Open enrollment was not a new strategy but the use of cable TV ads in a New England community was very different. The pastor reported an unexpected outcome as all the new students enrolled into the Christian school came from the cable advertisements. The pastor also reported that in the second school year they had enrolled almost 100 new students. Most of the students have since been saved and numerous parents have come to Christ as a result of this enrollment strategy. Creativity and a bold pursuit of enrollment are a part of the lessons learned.

Pastor Erven Burke has a strategic method of enrolling children. He states that he targets young families with children. When he visits door-to-door on Saturdays and visits the same neighborhood repeatedly and as the families begin to trust him some will enroll into the children's ministry. He also advertises on a country radio station that targets young families. The combination of these two strategies proves to be effective in enrolling children. The lessons learned are use media and the building of relationships with parents to enroll children into the ministry.

Pastor Bob Critchon has a creative strategy for children's ministry. When Pastor Critchon and his wife moved to Danbury, Connecticut to begin a new church ministry, Critchon had $150 per month of support to his name. As a bi-vocational pastor, he drove a public school bus full of elementary aged children every day. While driving the bus, he began to teach Bible verses and Bible songs to the public school children. He was able to win both the children and the parents to Christ and enroll some of them into the children's ministry. The church grew and eventually was able to open a Christian school for K-4 thru 12 grades. The lesson from Pastor Critchon was to be creative, especially when starting a new ministry, use every opportunity to do ministry, and be willing to relate to children as well as adults.

One major reason the project director came to Trinity Baptist Church in Jacksonville, Florida was because of a longstanding, though distant, relationship of 20 years with Pastor Tom Messer. Moving from the Northeast to the South and from a small church plant environment to a large, multi-staffed church held many cultural differences. Northeast churches are generally smaller, fewer paid staff, and many times the pastor must be bi-vocational in order to meet the needs of his family. One negative attribute of a smaller Northeastern church is that it may be almost exclusively led by the pastor and family members. This sometimes made it difficult for an unrelated church member to fit in or even have a place of service. A surprising factor, when moving to a southern church with over 2,000 members was a form of turf wars in the church. Sometimes there is an aversion to new people taking a place of leadership even when there is a long published list of volunteer positions that need to be filled. The cultural difference between the Northeast and the South within churches is that the Northeastern churches generally know there is a labor shortage. There tends to be more apathy in the southern church, as newcomers routinely seek involvement.

The most effective way to enroll children into the children's ministries at Trinity Baptist Church and Christian Academy were the bus ministry and the Christian school ministry. A couple of the procedures that the children's pastor, Paul Scott used in the children's ministry were to write the bus number on each of the children's hands so that each child would get back on the right bus when it was time to go home. When the children came off the buses to go to their Sunday school classes, each child would have to check into one of the kiosks located in the church and elementary school buildings before they could proceed to their class. There was also a big emphasis on the bus captains to get permission slips of new riders before the child could get on the bus. Scott also led Bible clubs at apartment complexes on Saturdays as well as Bible clubs at a public elementary school. The lesson learned from Scott was willingness to get creative in order to reach more children for Christ.

The interview with the principal at Trinity Christian Academy proved to be an encouraging one. The philosophy of ministry that Mrs. Teresa Haney brought to her 34 years of ministry at Trinity Christian Academy was most admirable. She used her office as a principal to win many parents and children to the Lord. As a result of the inferior public school system in Jacksonville, unsaved parents sought alternatives for their children. Haney states she would always present the gospel to the parents at the end of a school tour. All of Haney's teachers were soul-winners in and out of the classrooms. They would all make home visits and hospital visits to anyone remotely connected with the elementary school, and attend funerals.

Haney and her teachers would make every effort to invite the students to the Wednesday night AWANA program and to impress upon the parents the importance of church and the children's ministry. Many children and parents over the years have been baptized into membership at Trinity Baptist Church and become mature, productive church members.

Haney helped affirm the conviction that the Christian school is an evangelistic arm and a central part of the local church. The two do not work independently but in tandem with one another to accomplish the Great Commission and enroll as many children into the children's ministry as possible. The project director also found that Haney and her teachers saw their posts as a stewardship from the Lord. They saw themselves as more then professionals, but more as servants of the children that the Lord brought their way.

While visiting with one of the bus captains the project director discovered the long history of the bus ministry as well as the current state of the children's ministry. The changes in the children's ministry philosophy over the years have been significant. The church once sent 66 buses all over Jacksonville picking up children and in many instances parents. Now only six buses go into the community to pick up children. The feedback from every bus captain showed that they felt a sense of abandonment. The project director's assessment was as the bus ministry's culture had changed over the past 30-40 years, and that the church has seen diminishing returns from the bus ministry outreach.

This bus captain stressed that nothing can take the place of hard work or the building and maintaining of relationships. The bus ministry has about five years to reach families for the Lord and the church. This was the trend in previous decades. Now a bus captain may visit the home of a child riding the church bus about 50 times per year for

5 years. At the end of 250 faithful home visits the child is now in his or her mid-teenage years. Many times peer pressure and even pregnancy may lure the teenager away from the church. It appears that without the guidance, enforcement, and accompanying parents, the child has little likelihood of continuing in the children's or youth ministry. The most important part of this process is that the child would continue in their faith the rest of their lives, and to pass on their faith to the next generation.

The project director visited the bus route with one of the bus captain couples. What he learned was that not all the bus captains were well prepared to deal with children and parents past showing them how to be saved. In particular, the captains have not all been adequately trained in baptism presentations nor had the confidence to share why baptism is necessary following salvation. The weightier responsibility belongs to the children's pastor as he directly oversees the bus ministry. The remaining responsibility, as previously acknowledged in the post-training survey, is the believer's responsibility to the Great Commission.

The project director also spent time with another bus captain, while visiting the homes of the children on his bus route. This captain showed a good level of confidence while working with parents and children. Two observations were made by the project director. The first, which was a common theme among each of the bus captains, was that of discouragement. Without exception, each of the bus captains felt that both the children visited and the ones brought to church were not the highest priority. They also felt as volunteers there was a lack of needed support and encouragement. The project director suggested that the bus captain make appointments ahead of time on the phone, and with the parents of newly saved children that need to be baptized. This change may reduce frustration with missed appointments, and will open opportunities to present believers-baptism to the child and the parents, as well as more gospel presentations.

Remaining Things to be Accomplished

The project director will need to continue working through seven lesson plans with new people brought into the community class. The seven lesson model was designed to bring all the children's workers up to a level of personal confidence and biblical competence that will benefit the children and their parents. Another short lesson series that have yet to be written will continue focusing on teaching core biblical truths and training more leaders to reach and teach more children and parents. The objective will be to reach more children, while training more parents to be biblical mentors at home and apply more leadership in the children's ministry.

The project director will continue to visit the homes of children that have been saved and are in need of baptism. He will use these occasions to reach parents for the Lord, to present believers-baptism to the families, and to train the bus captains requesting follow-up visits with the contact's family or friends.

One of the challenges in recruiting new children's workers in this church is an aversion to reentering this area of ministry since so many have already served before. The project director is focused on reaching out to the church's newly saved adults and working to recruit them into the community class in order to disciple and train them for leadership in the children's ministry. As more leaders are trained, more children can be enrolled into the children's ministry. Part of this strategy will be to make home visits immediately following the baptism.

Job descriptions will have to be written for every position in the children's ministry. This will apply to volunteers and paid positions alike, although the paid positions may already have written job descriptions. The need for stronger leadership over the bus captains is essential for procedures, safety, legal issues, efficiencies in ministry, and to give direction when in the field. A children's ministry manual will need to be written. More pre and post surveys can be completed with workers so that better data is available regarding the training needs. Uniformity is imperative within the children's ministry so that as the sub-ministry organization grows, every leader will know where they fit in the chain of command.

APPENDIX A

PASTOR CHRIS ATKENSON INTERVIEW

Pastor Chris Atkenson Interview

1. What level of priority was the children's ministry at the beginning of your church ministry? 100% now.

2. Did the children's ministry come about intentionally or as a targeted ministry objective? A targeted objective.

3. What was the best strategy you found when you began enrolling children into the children's ministry? T.V., advertising, and website.

4. What mistakes were made when you first began enrolling children into the children's ministry? Lack of trained personnel.

5. What preparation or training of church members happened prior to establishing the children's ministry? The pastor did training seminars with teachers and workers. Procedures, discipline, story-telling, and personal soul winning are all topics that the pastor teaches.

6. What requirements, if any, did you place on children's workers and teachers prior to them becoming involved in the children's ministry? The pastor requires membership, adhering to the dress code, signing a commitment form, and faithful attendance to services. The church provides polo shirts for the teachers and workers.

7. Were background checks done? Were children's workers names checked against state websites of child offenders? The church does a statewide background check online. The pastor checks every one that fills out a visitor card on the state site.

8. How do you handle difficult children in the children's ministry? Send the child to sit with the parents or sit with a deacon. Talk with the parents. If that does not work suspend the child's permission to attend Sunday school for a week or two. If that does not fix the problem the child will not be permitted back to Sunday school.

9. How do you handle difficult parents of children in the children's ministry? Meet with parents. Tell them that the teachers and the pastor are running the Sunday school program and if they continue to disrupt other children they will have to go elsewhere.

10. How do you convey to the parents that they need to have a burden for their children's salvation? Preach on winning people to Christ. Present Christ to the parents.

11. How do you convince parents to make their children's spiritual development a high priority? "That's tough." Young people have to take spiritual charge of their own lives.

12. What percentage of your church budget is allocated to the children's ministry? Five percent to children and the youth. Thirty percent of the budget includes Christian school. How has that percentage changed over the years? The same to the present. The school should begin to pay more of its expenses in the future.

13. Has your children's ministry helped to increase enrollment at your Christian school? No, the other way around. The school enhanced the children's ministry. This church school practices open enrollment of their students.

14. How has your children's ministry helped the parents grow spiritually? As parents got involved it increased their spiritual growth.

15. How has the children's ministry helped to develop the rest of the church? The school has given the church more of a vision of what it can do for Christ. The church has done more baptisms as a result of the Christian school.

16. How would you measure the effectiveness of the children's ministry? It is operating at 75% effectiveness in the children, youth, and Christian school.

APPENDIX B

PASTOR ERVEN BURKE
INTERVIEW

Pastor Erven Burke Interview

1. What level of priority was the children's ministry at the beginning of your church ministry? It was the top priority. There was a nursery and Sunday school first and then a Christian school ministry.

2. Did the children's ministry come about intentionally or as a targeted ministry objective? It came about as a targeted ministry. The pastor went after young couples and families.

3. What was the best strategy you found when you began enrolling children into the children's ministry? The bus ministry began in 1974 the same year as the church. The church did door-to-door outreach every Saturday in the same neighborhoods. The families see you repeatedly so they learn to trust you.

4. What mistakes were made when you first began enrolling children into the children's ministry? The ratio of students to teachers was 40 to 1. Parents are more permissive today. Children run parents. The church had 300-400 children come in on buses. They did not have enough workers to manage the growth. There was a lack of teacher and worker training.

5. What preparation or training of church members happened prior to establishing the children's ministry? The pastor would have an orientation for new teachers and children's workers. He would let them observe the teacher in the class, and act as a helper for the teacher. They would learn the curriculum. And later, they were put in charge and taught a class. Monthly workers meetings were held before Wednesday night services or Sunday mornings before the Sunday school hour.

6. What requirements, if any, did you place on children's workers and teachers prior to them becoming involved in the children's ministry? They had to be saved and baptized, attend all services, tithe to the church, attend all training meetings, keep the dress code, and demonstrate good character.

7. Were background checks done? Were children's workers names checked against state websites of child offenders? Every teacher, worker, or volunteer must have background check completed prior to teaching or working with the children.

8. How do you handle difficult children in the children's ministry? First, the teacher handles it, then the Sunday school superintendent, and the last resort would be to go to the pastor.

9. How do you handle difficult parents of children in the children's ministry? Talk to them with the teacher, child, and others present to try to solve the problem.

10. How do you convey to the parents that they need to have a burden for their children's salvation? Show them from Scripture about their eternal soul, the Great Commission, and that none are exempt. Parents are responsible for their own soul. We challenge them to consider if they are saved and believe in the Bible.

11. How do you convince parents to make their children's spiritual development a high priority? Talk to the parents about their personal spiritual and devotional life. If the parent doesn't have a devotional life, neither will the children.

12. What percentage of your church budget is allocated to the children's ministry? Two percent. How has that percentage changed

over the years? It has been pretty steady for 37 years. It should be 10% of the church budget.

13. Has your children's ministry helped to increase enrollment at the Christian school? "In the beginning, yes. But now, no."

14. How has your children's ministry helped the parents grow spiritually? The parents see their children growing spiritually and that attracts them to want to learn more.

15. How has the children's ministry helped develop the rest of the church? It affects the parents in a positive way. The parents are moved emotionally by their own children's faith.

16. How would you measure the effectiveness of the children's ministry? It is weak at the present. It was stronger in the early days of the ministry. The church once had over 300 children in the children's church.

PASTOR BOB CRITCHTON INTERVIEW

Pastor Bob Critchton Interview

1. What level of priority was the children's ministry at the beginning of your church ministry? It was 40% children's outreach.

2. Did the children's ministry come about intentionally or as a targeted ministry objective? Yes, it was a targeted outreach.

3. What was the best strategy you found when you began enrolling children into the children's ministry? First, you have to love children. That is translated to the parents. The bus ministry and follow-up with the parents was very effective. The pastor drove a public school bus and taught Scripture and songs on the public school bus route.

4. What mistakes were made when you first began enrolling children into the children's ministry? The pastor said that none came to mind.

5. What preparation or training of church members happened prior to establishing the children's ministry? The pastor did an 18-week training series on soul-winning. They won family and friends of converts. They placed urgency into the hearts of every convert.

6. What requirements, if any, did you place on children's workers and teachers prior to them becoming involved in the children's ministry? They would be taught proper conduct and to be an example to the unsaved. They were taught to be good representatives for Christ.

7. Were background checks done? Were children's workers names checked against state websites of child offenders? Yes, they also trained the workers to have proper conduct around the children.

8. How do you handle difficult children in the children's ministry? They would deal with the child individually. Let them know that you love them, but they cannot distract the Sunday school. They would ask the child if they are having trouble at home. After a warning, the child would be told they cannot come back for a week or two.

9. How do you handle difficult parents of children in the children's ministry? They would explain to the parents why their child cannot misbehave and cause others to misbehave. They would tell the parents it would reinforce what the parents taught at home.

10. How do you convey to the parents that they need to have a burden for their children's salvation? They would teach the parent that the child is on loan from God, because the child has an eternal soul that may go to hell. Ask the parent, "How would you feel if your child went to hell?" Ask the parent, "How would you feel if your child went to prison?" Then make the spiritual connection.

11. How do you convince parents to make their children's spiritual development a high priority? Ask the parent, "What are your aspirations for your child?" Then make the spiritual connection to the question.

12. What percentage of your church budget is allocated to the children's ministry? Twenty-five percent of the church budget went to the children's ministry. How has that percentage changed over the years? The percentage stayed the same.

13. Has your children's ministry helped to increase enrollment at your Christian school? The bus ministry brought in families that in turn put their children into the Christian school.

14. How has your children's ministry helped the parents grow spiritually? The parents in response to the good spirit of the children wanted to grow too.

15. How has the children's ministry helped develop the rest of the church? A lot of children mean opportunities for adults to teach. The children bring a great atmosphere of excitement to the church.

16. How would you measure the effectiveness of the children's ministry? It was very effective. Every parent or grandparent wants to see their child memorize Scripture and learn songs.

CHILDREN'S PASTOR PAUL SCOTT INTERVIEW

Children's Pastor Paul Scott Interview

1. What level of priority is the children's ministry in the overall mission of the church ministry? Children's ministry is at the highest level along with missions and singles. Trinity Baptist Church is known in the community for putting a high emphasis on children's ministry.

2. Did the children's ministry come about intentionally or as a targeted ministry objective? Forty-five years ago Trinity Baptist had two Sunday school hours, Sunday school A and Sunday school B. The children's church originally was started to have a place for the children of the volunteer's children. Presently Trinity Baptist applies the children's church and Sunday school to reaching families for Christ.

3. What was the best strategy you found when you began enrolling children into the children's ministry? In 2013, the best enrollment strategy at Trinity Baptist Church is the bus ministry. The second best strategy for enrolling children is the Trinity Christian Academy. The curriculum used in the school is Abeka and Bob Jones. Currently, the enrollment at the academy is approximately 1,550 students.

4. What mistakes were made when you first began enrolling children into the children's ministry? The biggest mistake was having no detailed process. Now the teachers make three contacts, after the first visit to a Sunday school the prospect will get a postcard, second visit they will get a phone call. Not until the third visit will the prospect get a personal visit. All teachers report to the department's director. The director reports to the children's pastor.

5. What preparation or training do you provide the church members prior to making changes to the children's ministry? At the teacher

training meetings, held once a month, the implementation of new curriculum and processes takes place.

6. What requirements, if any, do you place on children's workers and teachers prior to them becoming involved in the children's ministry? They need to become members and then go through finger printing and a national background check.

7. How do you handle difficult children in the children's ministry? Individually. If the child is responsive they are discipled. If they are not responsive they are suspended. Ninety-eight percent of the children are responsive.

8. How do you handle difficult parents of children in the children's ministry? He would sit down with the parents, listen to them, and let them vent. He referenced the principle of Stephen Covey when Covey stated, "Seek first to understand them, then to be understood." [49]

9. How do you convey to the parents that they need to have a burden for their children's salvation? He brings out the parent's innate desire for their children to have a personal relationship with God.

10. How do you convince parents to make their children's spiritual development a high priority? Remind parent's that they want their children to obey, and thus, obedience is paramount to Christian teaching.

---

49 Stephen R. Covey, "The 7 Habits of Highly Effective People, Habit 5: Seek First to Understand, Then to Be Understood," The Community: Empowering Your Greatness, http://www.stephencovey.com/7habits/7habits-habit5.php (accessed October 1, 2013).

11. What percentage of your church budget is allocated to the children's ministry? Ten percent of a $3.5 million dollar budget is allocated to children's ministry, to include bus ministry (45-80 women and children ride the bus to church), AWANA, children's church, children's theater ($300K renovations), movie nights, women and children's center, and downtown rescue mission.

12. How has that percentage changed over the years? Ten percent currently. Prior to 2002, the budget may have been 20%, than with 45 leased buses we're going all over the city. The philosophy of outreach changed to where the church is doing more off site evangelism events, services, and personal evangelism. Currently, the ministry is putting more money per child into the children and less into the buses. The church is spending $300,000 budget dollars for about 280 children.

13. Has your children's ministry helped to raise enrollment in your Christian school? No. Bus riders are the exception to the rule. Of the 150 bus riders only about 2-3 children are enrolled in the Christian school.

14. How has your children's ministry helped the parents grow spiritually? The parent guide recaptures what was taught in the Sunday school class each week. Parents are asked to review the lesson with their child. Then the parent guides are to be turned in the next week.

15. How has the children's ministry helped develop the rest of the church? More people come to Christ at age 14 and below. A child living for God inspires adults and leads to revival first before revival ever gets to the adults in the church.

16. How would you measure the effectiveness of the children's ministry? The church is evaluated at a "B" as the children's ministries are healthy and growing, but need constant improvement.

17. How do the non-church member parents differ from the churched parents? The parents of the bus ministry are concerned but removed from the child's spiritual development. The church member parents are not perfect but are more invested and involved in the child's spiritual and academic development.

18. What is the current enrollment in the children's ministry of Trinity Baptist Church? As of October 1, 2013, the number of children enrolled in the children's ministry is 500. The current attendance of the children in the Sunday school and children's church is 280 children.

ELEMENTARY SCHOOL PRINCIPAL TERESA HANEY INTERVIEW

Elementary School Principal Teresa Haney Interview

1. How does the Christian school go about enrolling children into the school? When parents would contact the school they would be given a tour. The parents are asked about their church background and invited to Trinity Baptist. If they are not saved, the principal will witness to the parents. Information is given to the parents on enrollment and information is taken in on the child and parents. The parents then decide whether to enroll the child in the school.

2. Is the school open enrollment or closed? The school is open enrollment and evangelistic.

3. Does the school/church faculty/staff use the school to evangelize the students and parents? All of the faculty and staff are committed to using the ministry of the Christian school to evangelize parents and children, and enroll them into the Sunday school program.

4. What kinds of opportunities arise allowing you to evangelize the students and parents? First, with students they have Bible classes every day. They are taught Bible doctrine and stories. Each division of the school has their own chapel once a week. The students have the opportunity to talk to the teachers at any time regarding the Lord and salvation. The teachers many times are able to lead the children to the Lord. Second, the parents are invited to come to chapel every week with their child. The parents are also invited to come to special church services. Teachers make home visits where they are able to invite parents to church and witness to the parents in the home. During parent-conference the teachers and principal take the time to witness to the parents in addition to dealing with the academic issues.

5. What has been the best method of enrolling new students into the Christian school? Word of mouth has been the best source of new prospective students for the Christian school.

6. How has the school faculty been able to influence the parents with the importance of having the children in the Sunday school program? At the end of every chapel, the principal will ask the children, "Where are you going to be on Sunday?" The children all yell out, "Sunday school and church!" All the teachers encourage Sunday school, AWANA, and church attendance every week in the classrooms.

7. How does the local church staff work together with the Christian school faculty to assimilate the children and parents into the church and Sunday school? The children's pastor, Paul Scott, will sometimes teach at Kindergarten and Elementary chapel. The church youth director is in charge of the junior high and senior high chapel program. These men have regular opportunity to encourage children and parents to enroll/attend the Sunday school program and church services.

8. Does the school faculty see their position as an outreach of the local church? Absolutely, yes! Trinity Christian Academy is a ministry of Trinity Baptist Church. All faculty and staff of the academy are faithful members of Trinity Baptist Church.

9. Are the teachers trained and expected to persuade parents of their commitment to raise their children for the Lord? Yes, home visits are made regularly to talk with parents. Parent conferences are instrumental in persuading the parents to raise their children for the Lord. Also letters, emails, phone calls, and personal conversations are all part of mentoring the parents as they endeavor to raise godly children. While parents are helping their children

learn memory verses and passages for class it involves parents in the Word of God.

10. What is the best method to bridge the gap of the Christian school students to the Sunday school program? The teachers encourage the students to come to the Wednesday night AWANA program. When the children make friends in AWANA they are encouraged to visit the Sunday school. Teachers offer to sit with the parents in a Sunday school class and in church services.

SENIOR PASTOR INTERVIEW QUESTIONS

Senior Pastor Interview

1. What level of priority was the children's ministry at the beginning of your church ministry?

2. Did the children's ministry come about intentionally or as a targeted ministry objective?

3. What was the best strategy you found when you began enrolling children into the children's ministry?

4. What mistakes were made when you first began enrolling children into the children's ministry?

5. What preparation or training of church members happened prior to establishing the children's ministry?

6. What requirements, if any, did you place on children's workers and teachers prior to them becoming involved in the children's ministry?

7. Were background checks done? Were children's workers names checked against state websites of child offenders?

8. How do you handle difficult children in the children's ministry?

9. How do you handle difficult parents of children in the children's ministry?

10. How do you convey to the parents that they need to have a burden for their children's salvation?

11. How do you convince parents to make their children's spiritual development a high priority?

12. What percentage of your church budget is allocated to the children's ministry? How has that percentage changed over the years?

13. Has your children's ministry helped to increase enrollment your Christian school?

14. How has your children's ministry helped the parents grow spiritually?

15. How has the children's ministry helped develop the rest of the church?

16. How would you measure the effectiveness of the children's ministry?

CHILDREN'S PASTOR INTERVIEW QUESTIONS

Children's Pastor Interview

1. What level of priority is the children's ministry in the overall mission of the church ministry?

2. Did the children's ministry come about intentionally or as a targeted ministry objective?

3. What was the best strategy you found when you began enrolling children into the children's ministry?

4. What mistakes were made when you first began enrolling children into the children's ministry?

5. What preparation or training do you provide the church members prior to making changes to the children's ministry?

6. What requirements, if any, did you place on children's workers and teachers prior to them becoming involved in the children's ministry?

7. How do you handle difficult children in the children's ministry?

8. How do you handle difficult parents of children in the children's ministry?

9. How do you convey to the parents that they need to have a burden for their children's salvation?

10. How do you convince parents to make their children's spiritual development a high priority?

11. What percentage of your church budget is allocated to the children's ministry?

12. How has that percentage changed over the years?

13. Has your children's ministry helped to raise enrollment in your Christian school?

14. How has your children's ministry helped the parents grow spiritually?

15. How has the children's ministry helped develop the rest of the church?

16. How would you measure the effectiveness of the children's ministry?

17. How do the non-churched parents differ from the churched parents?

18. What is the current enrollment of the children's ministry at Trinity Baptist Church?

ELEMENTARY SCHOOL PRINCIPAL INTERVIEW QUESTIONS

Elementary School Principal's Questions

1. How does the Christian school go about enrolling children into the school?

2. Is the school open enrollment or closed?

3. Does the school/church faculty/staff use the school to evangelize the students and parents?

4. What kinds of opportunities arise allowing you to evangelize the students and parents?

5. What has been the best method of enrolling new students into the Christian school?

6. How has the school faculty been able to influence the parents with the importance of having the children in the Sunday school program?

7. How does the local church staff work together with the Christian school faculty to assimilate the children and parents into the church and Sunday school?

8. Does the school faculty see their position as an outreach of the local church?

9. Are the teachers trained and expected to persuade parents of their commitment to raise their children for the Lord?

10. What is the best method to bridge the gap of the Christian school students to the Sunday school program?

COMMUNITY GROUP BIBLE STUDY CLASS: LESSON 1

Community Group Bible Study Class: Lesson 1

Great Commission and Children's Ministry

Project Director: Andrew Knight

Matthew 28:18-20 "And Jesus came and spake unto them, saying, All power is given unto me in heaven and in earth. 19 Go ye therefore, and teach all nations, baptizing them in the name of the Father, and of the Son, and of the Holy Ghost: 20 Teaching them to observe all things whatsoever I have commanded you: and, lo, I am with you alway, even unto the end of the world. Amen."

Group Discussion Questions:

1. Based on these verses, what are the three objectives of the believer on earth?
   A. _____
   B. _____
   C. _____

2. Name four ways that teaching can be applied.
   A. _____
   B. _____
   C. _____
   D. _____

Deuteronomy 6:4-8 "Hear, O Israel: The LORD our God is one LORD: 5 And thou shalt love the LORD thy God with all thine heart, and with all thy soul, and with all thy might. 6 And these words, which I command thee this day, shall be in thine heart: And thou shalt teach them diligently unto thy children, and shalt talk of them when thou sittest in thine house, and when thou walkest by the way, and when thou liest down, and when thou risest up. 8 And thou shalt bind them for a sign upon thine hand, and they shall be as frontlets between thine eyes."

Group Discussion Questions:

3. Based on these verses what is the motivation for our relationship with the Lord?
   A. _____
   B. _____
   C. _____

4. What is the scope of the teaching setting?
   A. _____
   B. _____
   C. _____
   D. _____

5. Who does this teaching apply too?
   A. _____
   B. _____
   C. _____

Potential Applications for the Group:

1. Personal soul-winning; work a bus route.
2. Discuss baptism with a child that is newly converted, along with the parents.
3. Witness to parents of the children on the bus route.

4. Ask children and parents for F.R.A.N., (Friends, Relatives, Associates, and Neighbors) contacts that may be visited and encouraged to come to the Sunday school and church.
5. Commit to learn the Word of God.
6. Commit to teach others in the Word of God.
7. Commit to mentor new believers.
8. Seek to counsel others with biblical principles.

COMMUNITY GROUP BIBLE STUDY CLASS: LESSON 2

Community Group Bible Study Class: Lesson 2

Great Commission and Children's Ministry

Project Director: Andrew Knight

Mark 16:15 "And he said unto them, Go ye into all the world, and preach the gospel to every creature."

Group Discussion Questions:

1. Based on this verse of Scripture, who does this apply too? Is the "ye" singular or plural in this passage?

   A. _____

   B. _____

Mark 16:9-14 "Now when Jesus was risen early the first day of the week, he appeared first to Mary Magdalene, out of whom he had cast seven devils. And she went and told them that had been with him, as they mourned and wept. And they, when they had heard that he was alive, and had been seen of her, believed not. After that he appeared in another form unto two of them, as they walked, and went into the country. And they went and told it unto the residue: neither believed they them. Afterward he appeared unto the eleven as they sat at meat, and upbraided them with their unbelief and hardness of heart, because they believed not them which had seen him after he was risen."

2. What was the spiritual state of Jesus' disciples when He gave this charge?

   A. _____

   B. _____

   C. _____

Group Discussion Questions:

3. Was this text describing people that are not even saved?

   _____

4. Were the disciples saying that they didn't believe in the resurrection? And yet they believed on Christ as the Messiah during His 3½ earthly ministry. What are the possible causes for the carnal reaction that Christ is alive?

   A. _____
   B. _____
   C. _____

5. What excuses do people give for not actively being involved in winning the lost?

   A. _____
   B. _____
   C. _____

6. What are some reasons why every Christian can and should be engaged in winning the lost?

   A. _____
   B. _____
   C. _____

Potential Applications for the Group:

1. Every believer must recognize their individual and corporate responsibility to do what they can to help carry out the Great Commission.

2. Every believer must understand that Great Commission work is to be committed to in spite of difficult circumstances or even emotional distress.

3. The believer must guard ones heart from unbelief and hardness of heart.

4. Faithfulness to witness for the Lord requires one to overcome the fear of rejection in order to be a witness for the Lord.

5. Christians must train their hearts to overcome the fear of failure.

COMMUNITY GROUP BIBLE STUDY CLASS: LESSON 3

Community Group Bible Study Class: Lesson 3

Great Commission and Children's Ministry

Project Director: Andrew Knight

Matthew 19:14 "But Jesus said, Suffer little children, and forbid them not, to come unto me: for of such is the kingdom of heaven."

Group Discussion Questions:

1. What does this verse teach us about God's priority to reach children?

_____

_____

_____

2. Why do you think God equates children with the kingdom of heaven?

_____

_____

_____

_____

3. Why do you think the culture values are different then the kingdom values?

_____

_____

_____

Proverbs 22:6 "Train up a child in the way he should go: and when he is old, he will not depart from it."

Group Discussion Questions:

4. Why do you think children are apt to continue in their faith for the remainder of their lives?

_____

_____

_____

5. What reason might God view children as a higher priority in relationship to the Great Commission?

_____

_____

_____

6. How do you think children view the gospel differently than adults?

_____

_____

_____

Psalms 34:11 "Come, ye children, hearken unto me: I will teach you the fear of the LORD?"

Group Discussion Questions:

7. Why do you think King David took the time to teach the children about the Lord?

_____

_____

_____

8. What do you think it means to be taught the "fear of the Lord?"

_____

_____

_____

9. What qualities do you think King David had exhibited while teaching the children the fear of the Lord?"

A. _____

B. _____

10. What do you thing the spiritual benefits are in teaching children? (in contrast to teaching adults)

A. _____

B. _____

C. _____

Potential Applications for the Group:

1. As Christians we must think in terms of kingdom values as it relates to children.
2. As adult men we should practice child-like faith in our daily lives.
3. As maturing followers and servants of Christ we must train our minds and thinking to resist what the unsaved sub-culture values and embrace the kingdom values.
4. As Christians we must realize that children have longer to live and serve the Lord. We must refocus our attention on reaching children for the Lord.
5. Keep in mind while dealing with children that they see the world and the gospel differently than adults.
6. As an adult make a mental note to be humble enough to invest time ministering to children.

7. As Christians we need to practice the presence of God by acknowledging the fear of the Lord in our personal lives.

8. As a Christian we must forefront in our minds the spiritual benefits and blessings of working with children.

COMMUNITY GROUP BIBLE STUDY CLASS: LESSON 4

Community Group Bible Study Class: Lesson 4

Great Commission and Children's Ministry

Project Director: Andrew Knight

Matthew 19:14 "But Jesus said, Suffer little children, and forbid them not, to come unto me: for of such is the kingdom of heaven."

Plan of Salvation

Children's ministry is a process and an ongoing process always begins with evangelism. When presenting the gospel to children, it is important to keep the gospel presentation as simple as possible. It is also important when making illustrations to make them in terms that children can understand.

Step One: Children need to be made to understand that they our sinners that they have sinned against God. And that if they want to know for sure that they will go to heaven one day, they need to respond to God's offer of forgiveness and salvation. The best way to illustrate this when working with children is to make the connection between the parent–child relationships. Children get this!

- **Romans 3:23** "For all have sinned, and come short of the glory of God;"

- **Romans 6:23** "For the wages of sin is death; but the gift of God is eternal life through Jesus Christ our Lord."

- **Romans 5:8** "But God commendeth his love toward us, in that, while we were yet sinners, Christ died for us."

- **Romans 5:12** "Wherefore, as by one man sin entered into the world, and death by sin; and so death passed upon all men, for that all have sinned:"

Group Discussion Questions:

1. What are two things that can be done to help understanding while teaching children?

   A. _____

   B. _____

Step Two: After giving Scripture to show the child from the Bible you will then want to illustrate the point. This will draw the child into the conversation even more.

- Ask the child, "Have you ever disobeyed your mother or father?"

- Then ask the child, "Don't you want to go to be with Jesus someday?"

- You can also ask, "Wouldn't you like to be in heaven one day with other family members?"

Step Three: The child needs to know that Jesus loves them. The point that a child has sinned is a far different point then that God is a good, loving, and forgiving God. One must impress upon the child that God loves them in a profound way.

- Ask the child, "Your mom and dad love you don't they?"

- Ask the child, "Do you understand that God loves you even more than anyone else could?"

Group Discussion Questions:

2. What do illustrations do for the child's learning?

   A. _____

   B. _____

3. What other techniques can the teacher employ to draw the child into the conversation?

   A. _____

   B. _____

4. What are two possible outcomes from asking pre-planned questions?

   A. _____

   B. _____

Step Four: Show the child from the Bible how much God loves them.

- **John 3:16** "For God so loved the world, that he gave his only begotten Son, that whosoever believeth in him should not perish, but have everlasting life."

- **Romans 5:5** "And hope maketh not ashamed; because the love of God is shed abroad in our hearts by the Holy Ghost which is given unto us."

Step Five: The child needs to be led in prayer to ask Jesus into their heart.

- **Romans 10:10** "For with the heart man believeth unto righteousness; and with the mouth confession is made unto salvation."

- **Romans 10:13** "For whosoever shall call upon the name of the Lord shall be saved."

Step Six: Pray "heaven's prayer" with the child, and ask them to pray out loud with you.

Prayer: "Dear Lord, I know that I am a sinner. And I know that You sent Jesus to die on the cross for my sins. I know that You raised Jesus from the grave. Now, I ask Jesus to forgive all my sins, and to come into my heart. I trust You alone to take me to heaven one day. I thank You for saving me. In Jesus' name, Amen!"

Step Seven: Give the child a reason from Scripture how they know that once saved God keeps them saved and will take those saved to heaven one day.

- **John 10:27-29** "My sheep hear my voice, and I know them, and they follow me:
  And I give unto them eternal life; and they shall never perish, neither shall any man pluck them out of my hand. My Father, which gave them me, is greater than all; and no man is able to pluck them out of my Father's hand."

- **I John 5:11-13** "And this is the record, that God hath given to us eternal life, and this life is in his Son. He that hath the Son hath life; and he that hath not the Son of God hath not life. These things have I written unto you that believe on the name of the Son of God; that ye may know that ye have eternal life, and that ye may believe on the name of the Son of God."

- Ask the child, "Based upon these two passages, do you understand that God will never leave you now that you are His child?"

Group Discussion Questions:

5. What is the main characteristic of God that you want to empress upon a child?

   _____

6. What is the name of the prayer that you need to lead the child in?

   _____

7. What is the scriptural reason that one would need to give a child after the child prays to ask Jesus into their heart?

   _____

Potential Applications for the Group:

1. Make the commitment to learn the plan of salvation outline so that you may be confident to present the gospel anytime and anywhere.

2. Commit to memory the above verses of Scripture so that they can be communicated whenever an opportunity avails itself to share the gospel.

3. Commit to memory the above questions so that your conversation with a child flows smoothly and logically.

4. Make a commitment to reaching and sharing the gospel with children.

COMMUNITY GROUP BIBLE STUDY CLASS: LESSON 5

Community Group Bible Study Class: Lesson 5

Great Commission and Children's Ministry

Project Director: Andrew Knight

Acts 2:41 "Then they that gladly received his word were baptized: and the same day there were added unto them about three thousand souls."

Baptism— The Second Step of Obedience to the Lord
The conflict you may have right away when dealing with children and baptism after conversion is to clearly communicate the different motivation to be saved versus the motivation to be baptized. The connection between baptism and salvation is that one must be saved before they can be baptized. The disconnect between salvation and baptism is that the former is to receive God's gift of eternal life the later has nothing to do with gaining eternal life. Baptism is the beginning of stewardship to the Lord.

Step One: Talk to the child about the difference between a gift and obedience. Say to the child, "Do you pay your parents for a birthday or Christmas gift?" Then ask the child, "Do your parents expect you to obey them?" The contrast between asking Jesus into their heart and being baptized will then be made.

- **Ephesians 2:8-9** "For by grace are ye saved through faith; and that not of yourselves: it is the gift of God: Not of works, lest any man should boast."

- **Titus 3:5** "Not by works of righteousness which we have done, but according to his mercy he saved us, by the washing of regeneration, and renewing of the Holy Ghost;"

Step Two: You will want to give the child a couple examples from the Bible of those that have followed the Lord in believers-baptism. This will give the child a good example to follow as they take this second step of obedience to the Lord.

- **Acts 8:12** "But when they believed Philip preaching the things concerning the kingdom of God, and the name of Jesus Christ, they were baptized, both men and women."

- **Acts 18:8** "And Crispus, the chief ruler of the synagogue, believed on the Lord with all his house; and many of the Corinthians hearing believed, and were baptized."

Step Three: The broader reason of baptism should be explained to the child in the context of believers-baptism being at the center of Great Commission. You might talk to the child in terms of their relationship with their parents. The connection between obeying parents and obeying the Lord is an easy connection for the child to make.

- **Matthew 28:19** "Go ye therefore, and teach all nations, baptizing them in the name of the Father, and of the Son, and of the Holy Ghost:"

- **Acts 10:48** "And he said unto them, Ye know how that it is an unlawful thing for a man that is a Jew to keep company, or come unto one of another nation; but God hath shewed me that I should not call any man common or unclean."

Step Four: It is good to communicate the process of baptism to a child by illustrating what the process entails and what the baptism process represents. Explaining the baptism process to a child should relieve some anxiety of what is an unfamiliar experience, so they will know what to expect and feel safe proceeding with the baptism. What the baptism represents is the death, burial, and resurrection of Jesus Christ. It is important when communicating this to the child that you illustrate it clearly.

- **Matthew 3:16** "And Jesus, when he was baptized, went up straightway out of the water: and, lo, the heavens were opened unto him, and he saw the Spirit of God descending like a dove, and lighting upon him:"

- **Acts 8:38** "And he commanded the chariot to stand still: and they went down both into the water, both Philip and the eunuch; and he baptized him."

- **Colossians 2:12** "Buried with him in baptism, wherein also ye are risen with him through the faith of the operation of God, who hath raised him from the dead."

Step Five: When dealing with children and their parents it is not good to pressure them into taking the step of baptism. Remember that it is a process and every believer grows incrementally. When seeking a commitment from children and their parents ask for a series of commitments. One way to do this is to ask the question, "Do you understand?" This question can be asked a number of times throughout the conversation. The final point to impress upon the child and parents is that baptism for the new Christian is a public profession of faith. The child being baptized benefits from exercising their faith; while the local church is encouraged by a child's trust in Christ as their personal Savior. The local church then has the opportunity to encourage the child that has been baptized and welcome them into the family of God.

- **Acts 8:12** "But when they believed Philip preaching the things concerning the kingdom of God, and the name of Jesus Christ, they were baptized, both men and women."

- **Acts 16:33** "And he took them the same hour of the night, and washed their stripes; and was baptized, he and all his, straightway."

Step Six: While making home visits with families it is important to ask the parents after a baptism presentation, "Do you have any questions regarding believers-baptism?" Whatever the parent answers, this is the appropriate time to ask about their salvation. If they are already saved, ask the parents, "Is there any reason you would not want to be baptized along with your child?" If the parents don't know if they are saved take the time to present the gospel to them. This is kingdom opportunity time. Take it!

Step Seven: The last objective to accomplish while making a home visit is to ask the children, "Are there friends of yours that you would like us to invite to your Sunday school class or program?" Then to the parents ask, "Do you have friends, neighbors, or co-workers that might need special prayer or just a friendly visit?" Children's workers should always carry note cards with them so that they can write down new contacts for the children's ministry.

Group Discussion Questions:

1. What is the difference in a child's motivation to be saved versus to be baptized?

_____

_____

_____

2. Why baptism is called the "second step" of obedience to the Lord?

_____

_____

3. What is the significance of using a "gift from parents" when explaining the difference between salvation versus baptism to a child?

_____

_____

_____

4. What significance does Matthew 28:19 have with regard to baptism?

_____

_____

5. What two things are accomplished when a new Christian follows the Lord in believer's baptism?
   A. _____
   B. _____

6. What two things should the children's worker ask while finishing up a home visit?
   A. _____
   B. _____

Potential Applications for the Group:

1. Memorize the "planned questions" relating to baptism so you can use these questions when dealing with children and parents.
2. Memorize the Scriptures regarding baptism, as a children's worker you may be reading upside down so the child or parent can read along as baptism is presented.

3. Use baptism examples so that this becomes real to the child and parents.

4. Meditate on Scripture recognizing that after salvation baptism is central in the Great Commission.

5. Make home visits this week with someone that is comfortable presenting believer's baptism to children and parents.

6. Illustrate with your hands the death, burial, and resurrection of Jesus Christ while communicating the symbolism of baptism to at least one child and parent this week.

7. While presenting baptism this week also present the gospel to at least one parent or set of parents. This can be called "backing into the gospel."

8. This week ask at least one child and one parent for names and addresses of other children or adults that you can visit.

COMMUNITY GROUP BIBLE STUDY CLASS: LESSON 6

Community Group Bible Study Class: Lesson 6

Great Commission and Children's Ministry

Project Director: Andrew Knight

II Timothy 2:2 "And the things that thou hast heard of me among many witnesses, the same commit thou to faithful men, who shall be able to teach others also."

Teaching and Training: An Ongoing Objective

Step One: Understand that the biblical model for leadership is faithful believers that can become a disciple of Jesus Christ and entrusted with God's Word to in turn disciple another faithful believer.

- **I Samuel 16:7** "But the LORD said unto Samuel, Look not on his countenance, or on the height of his stature; because I have refused him: for the LORD seeth not as man seeth; for man looketh on the outward appearance, but the LORD looketh on the heart."

- **I Corinthians 11:1** "Be ye followers of me, even as I also am of Christ."

Step Two: Understand that the Lord's work is not based upon the economy of the world, but rather the economy of God's kingdom. The qualities and actions that are highly esteemed by the world are not the same qualities and actions that are esteemed by the Lord.

- **Matthew 5:19** "Whosoever therefore shall break one of these least commandments, and shall teach men so, he shall be called the least in the kingdom of heaven: but whosoever shall do and teach them, the same shall be called great in the kingdom of heaven."

- **Mark 10:14-15** "But when Jesus saw it, he was much displeased, and said unto them, Suffer the little children to come unto me, and forbid them not: for of such is the kingdom of God. Verily I say unto you, Whosoever shall not receive the kingdom of God as a little child, he shall not enter therein."

Step Three: Leadership in ministry comes about when two key biblical principles are applied. The first principle is "follow-ship." The second principle is to dominate fears.

- **Matthew 16:24** "Then said Jesus unto his disciples, If any man will come after me, let him deny himself, and take up his cross, and follow me."

- **II Timothy 1:7** "For God hath not given us the spirit of fear; but of power, and of love, and of a sound mind."

Step Four: Leadership requires biblical growth in the Word of God and in stretching yourself to more fully apply your God-given talents and abilities to the ministry opportunities that come your way. A clear way to view service and love for God are how you serve people. Spiritual growth comes by study, and many times comes best by having accountability in your life.

- **Acts 22:3** "I am verily a man which am a Jew, born in Tarsus, a city in Cilicia, yet brought up in this city at the feet of Gamaliel, and taught according to the perfect manner of the law of the fathers, and was zealous toward God, as ye all are this day."

- **II Timothy 2:15** "Study to shew thyself approved unto God, a workman that needeth not to be ashamed, rightly dividing the word of truth."

Step Five: The application part of ministry is engaging with parents and children in the first and second steps of their spiritual walk. This may require light biblical counsel with the parents, picking up and dropping off the children, making visits on Saturdays or any time a need comes up with a family. It takes continual follow-up, including visits and phone calls.

- **Luke 14:23** "And the lord said unto the servant, Go out into the highways and hedges, and compel them to come in, that my house may be filled. (Though this passage refers to the marriage super of the Lamb the application can be made to evangelism).

- **Proverbs 11:30** "The fruit of the righteous is a tree of life; and he that winneth souls is wise."

Group Discussion Questions:

1. Based upon II Timothy 2:2 what does this passage teach whom we should entrust with passing on the gospel message?

   _____ _ _

   _____

   _____

2. Explain how the world's economy differs from the economy of God's kingdom?

_____

_____

_____

3. What are the two biblical leadership principles that were mentioned in this lesson?

A. _____

B. _____

4. What are the two first steps taken in a person's spiritual walk with the Lord?

A. _____

B. _____

Potential Applications for the Group:

1. Invite 6-8 faithful believers to the teacher-training Bible study next week.
2. Begin viewing other believers on the fruit of their heart rather than their outside appearance or life station.
3. Begin to view yourself not as a leader of men but rather a follower of Christ.
4. Begin to concisely view your life in terms of the economy of the kingdom of God.
5. Begin to concisely view God as bigger than any fear of man.
6. Be willing to put yourself in a place of ministry where you may not feel comfortable but where God can stretch and mold you for His service and glory.
7. Engage children and parents this week in the two steps of obedience to Him.

COMMUNITY GROUP BIBLE STUDY CLASS: LESSON 7

Community Group Bible Study Class: Lesson 7

Great Commission and Children's Ministry

Project Director: Andrew Knight

Mathew 16:18 "And I say also unto thee, That thou art Peter, and upon this rock I will build my church; and the gates of hell shall not prevail against it."

Local Church Membership—Essential to the Children's Ministry

Principle One: The local church is God's program and institution for getting the gospel to the whole world. It is the local church that connects the gospel to the world where converts are baptized into membership. It is the institution that was founded upon Jesus Christ, and recorded in the Gospels, the book of Acts, and the Epistles.

- **Matthew 3:2; 5-6** "And saying, Repent ye: for the kingdom of heaven is at hand.; Then went out to him Jerusalem, and all Judaea, and all the region round about Jordan, And were baptized of him in Jordan, confessing their sins."

- **Acts 2:41** "Then they that gladly received his word were baptized: and the same day there were added unto them about three thousand souls."

  A. The local church will rejoice when children come to a saving knowledge of Jesus Christ.
  B. The local church is whose membership a new convert is baptized into.
  C. The local church is where soul-winners are sent out from. It is the local church where the believers gather, worship, and serve together.

109

Principle Two: Service to the Lord is a large part of worship and much of what Christians will be doing in heaven. Service to the Lord is a command of the Lord. Service to the Lord is seen in the Great Commission and throughout Scripture. It is impossible to love the Lord without service to Him.

- **I Samuel 12:24** "Only fear the LORD, and serve him in truth with all your heart: for consider how great things he hath done for you."

- **John 12:26** "If any man serve me, let him follow me; and where I am, there shall also my servant be: if any man serve me, him will my Father honour."

  A. Service to the Lord is inclusive of involvement in the children's ministry.
  B. Following the Lord is to love and reach children that He loves.
  C. Serving the Lord through the local church helps to accomplish His will in any one place.

Principle Three: The stewardship of a Christian's life includes your time, abilities, and personal resources. All that is given to every believer is an opportunity to bring glory to the Lord.

- **Deuteronomy 6:5** "And thou shalt love the LORD thy God with all thine heart, and with all thy soul, and with all thy might."

- **Colossians 3:23** "And whatsoever ye do, do it heartily, as to the Lord, and not unto men;"

- **Leviticus 27:30** "And all the tithe of the land, whether of the seed of the land,   or of the fruit of the tree, is the LORD'S: it is holy unto the LORD."

Group Discussion Questions:

1. What is the main institution that God uses to evangelize the world?

   _____

2. What step of obedience places a new convert into local church membership?

   _____

3. What are the two biblical requirements for church membership?
   A. _____
   B. _____

4. According to the second principle, worship is part of _____ to the Lord.

5. Based upon I Samuel 12:24 we serve the Lord in _____, with what part of our hearts? _____

6. According to John 12:26, who will the Father honor?

   _____

7. Principle Three teaches the stewardship of what three things?
   A. _____
   B. _____
   C. _____

Potential Applications for the Group:

1. Be involved in getting children baptized after they are saved.
2. Seek opportunities and different ways you can serve people.
3. Be a faithful steward of all the time, abilities, and resources.

COMMUNITY GROUP
BIBLE STUDY ANSWERS: 1

Community Group Bible Study Answers: Lesson 1

Answers:

1. Based on these verses what are the three objectives for the believer on earth?
   B. Evangelize the lost. Baptize the converts.
   C. Disciple all believers.

2. Name four ways that teaching can be applied?
   A. Evangelize.
   B. Disciple.
   C. Teaching.
   D. Counseling.

3. Based on these verses what is the motivation for our relationship with the Lord?
   A. Love the Lord.
   B. With all your soul.
   C. With all your might.

4. What is the scope of the teaching?
   A. Sitting in the house.
   B. Walking in the way.
   C. Lying down.
   D. Rising up.

5. Who does this teaching apply too?
   A. Children.
   B. Wife.
   C. Circle of influence.

COMMUNITY GROUP BIBLE STUDY ANSWERS: 2

Community Group Bible Study Answers: Lesson 2

Answers:

1. Based on this verse who does this apply to? Is the "ye" singular or plural in this passage?
   A. Every believer and every local church.
   B. Plural – everyone.

2. What is the spiritual state of Jesus' disciples when He gave this charge?
   A. Morning and weeping.
   B. Unbelief.
   C. Hardness of heart.

3. Was the text describing people that are not even saved?
   Answer: No

4. Were the disciples saying that they didn't believe in the resurrection? And yet they believed on Christ as the Messiah during His 3 ½ year earthly ministry. What are the possible causes for the carnal reaction that Christ is alive?
   A. Life challenges.
   B. Emotional trials.
   C. Anger because of the death of a loved one.

5. What excuses do people give for not actively being involved in winning the lost?
   A. Fear of rejection.
   B. Fear of failure.
   C. Unwanted responsibility.

6. What are some reasons why every Christian can and should be engaged in winning the lost?

    A. We are commanded to win the lost.

    B. We are obligated to give the gospel to the lost.

    C. We should win crowns and give the glory to Christ.

COMMUNITY GROUP
BIBLE STUDY ANSWERS: 3

Community Group Bible Study Answers: Lesson 3

Answers:

1. What does the verse teach us about God's priority to reach children?
   Answer: Jesus saw the innocence of children and their willingness to trust Jesus.

2. Why do you think God equates children with the kingdom of heaven?
   Answer: Children are innocent and their child-like faith is endearing to Jesus.

3. Why do you think the culture values are different then the kingdom values?
   Answer: The culture is godless, and the kingdom is all about God.

4. Why do you think children are apt to continue in their faith for the remainder of their lives?
   Answer: One Bible reason is because of eternal security. Another reason is that habits are formed during childhood.

5. What reason might God view children as a higher priority in relationship to the Great Commission?
   Answer: One reason is that children have longer to live for the Lord; therefore, children have longer to serve the Lord.

6. How do you think children view the gospel differently than adults?
   Answer: Children may view the gospel in terms of being loved by the heavenly Father, while adults my see the gospel as a remedy for sins and life problems.

7. Why do you think King David took the time to teach the children about the Lord?
Answer: King David knew that the children would grow up to be God-fearing adults.

8. What do you think it means to be taught the fear of the Lord?
Answer: The fear of the Lord could include honor, respect, reverence, and worship.

9. What qualities do you think King David exhibited while teaching the children the fear of the Lord?
A. Godliness.
B. Humility.

10. What do you think the spiritual benefits are in teaching children? (in contrast to teaching adults)
A. Children learn quicker.
B. Fewer obstacles to faith.
C. A natural love for Jesus.

COMMUNITY GROUP
BIBLE STUDY ANSWERS: 4

Community Group Bible Study Answers: Lesson 4

Answers:

1. What are two things that can be done to help understanding while teaching children?
   A. Simplicity.
   B. Illustrations.

2. What do illustrations do for a child's learning?
   A. It draws the child into the Bible lesson.
   B. It helps the child envision the Bible story.

3. What other techniques can the teacher employ to draw the child into the conversation?
   A. Ask pre-planned questions.
   B. Tailor illustrations to the child.

4. What are the two possible outcomes of pre-planned questions?
   A. It keeps the child focused on the salvation message.
   B. They will help to lead the child to trust in the Lord.

5. What is the main characteristic of God that you want to impress upon a child?
   Answer: The love of God.

6. What is the name of the prayer that you need to lead the child?
   Answer: "heaven's prayer"

7. What is the scriptural reason that you would need to give after the child prayed to ask Jesus into their hearts?
   Answer: An assurance of salvation.

COMMUNITY GROUP
BIBLE STUDY ANSWERS: 5

Community Group Bible Study Answers: Lesson 5

Answers:

1. What is the difference in a child's motivation to be saved verses to be baptized?
   Answer: Accepting God's grace vs. obedience to the Lord is a matter of stewardship.

2. Why is baptism called the "second step" of obedience to the Lord?
   Answer: Trusting the Lord is the first step of obedience.

3. What is the significance of using a "gift from parents" when explaining the difference between salvation verses baptism to a child?
   Answer: A child doesn't pay for a gift, he just receives a gift.

4. What significance does Matthew 28:19 have with regard to baptism?
   Answer: Baptism is a central part of the Great Commission.

5. What two things are accomplished when a new Christian follows the Lord in believer's baptism?
   A. The new believer expresses their faith.
   B. Believers in the church are encouraged.

6. What two things should the children's worker ask while finishing up a home visit?
   A. Ask the child if they have friends they want to have in Sunday school with them.
   B. Ask the parents if they have family or friends that need special prayer or a friend's visit.

COMMUNITY GROUP
BIBLE STUDY ANSWERS: 6

Community Group Bible Study Answers: Lesson 6

Answers:

1. Based upon II Timothy 2:2, what does this passage teach whom we should entrust with passing on the gospel message?
   Answer: Those believers who fear the Lord bear fruit of righteousness and   character.

2. Explain how the world's economy differs from the economy of God's kingdom?
   Answer: The kingdom of this world is humanism and selfish gain. The kingdom of God is about reaching children and adults with child-like faith.

3. What are the two biblical leadership principles that were mentioned in this lesson?
   A. Follow-ship.
   B. Conquer fears.

4. What are the two first steps taken in one's spiritual walk with the Lord?
   A. Trust Christ as Savior.
   B. Follow the Lord in believer's baptism.

COMMUNITY GROUP BIBLE STUDY ANSWERS: 7

Community Group Bible Study Answers: Lesson 7

Answers:

1. What is the main institution that God uses to evangelize the world?
   Answer: The local church.

2. What step of obedience places a new convert into local church membership?
   Answer: Believer's baptism.

3. What are the two biblical requirements for church membership?
   A. Salvation.
   B. Baptism.

4. According to the second principle, worship is part of _____ to the Lord.
   Answer: Service.

5. Based upon I Samuel 12:24 we serve the Lord in _____, with what part of our hearts? _____.
   A. Truth.
   B. All.

6. According to John 12:26, who will the Father honor?
   _____
   Answer: Those that serve Him.

7. Principle Three teaches the stewardship of what three things?
   A. Time.
   B. Abilities.
   C. Reserves.

COMMUNITY CLASS PRE-TRAINING SURVEY

Community Class Pre-Training Survey

The Gospel

1. At what point must a person get to in their lives before they can be saved?

   _____

2. What two things will a person need to act upon in order to be saved?

   A. _____

   B. _____

3. What is the central theme of the gospel?

   _____

   _____

4. What does "whosoever salvation" mean to you?

   _____

   _____

   _____

5. Can children be saved? _____

   Can children die and go to hell if they were not saved during their lifetime? _____.

Great Commission

1. Is the Great Commission for the church, the pastor, or for every believer?

   _____

2. Does the Great Commission include salvation, baptism, Christian education, or just salvation?

   _____

3. Is the Great Commission for every generation? _____
   When did it begin? _____
   When does the Great Commission end? _____

4. Is there urgency to the Great Commission? _____
   If yes, why? _____

5. What are some of the rewards and blessings that come with having a part in the Great Commission work?

   _____

   _____

Devotional Life

1. Do you have a regular Bible reading schedule on a daily basis?

   _____

2. How would you describe your private prayer life?

   _____

3. Define worship.

   _____

   _____

4. Would you describe your spiritual life as growing, stationary, or in a reversal?

   _____

5. Is your devotional life spent with a friend, spouse, or by yourself?

_____

Leadership Abilities

1. Would you consider yourself to be a follower or a leader?

_____

2. Do you believe leaders are born or developed?

_____

3. Do you see leadership as a gift or a skill?

_____

4. If you had the opportunity to develop your leadership abilities would you?

_____

5. When leadership opportunities avail themselves are you likely to take advantage of them?

_____

Spiritual Gifts

1. What would you consider your spiritual gift to be? A teacher, prophet (preacher),or helps? _____

2. How do you think that your spiritual gift fits into the Great Commission work?

_____

_____

_____

3. Do you see your gift as a stewardship in the Great Commission work?

_____

Please explain.

_____

_____

4. How do you think you should go about developing your spiritual gift?

_____

_____

5. Would you like to be able to help others develop their spiritual gifts?

_____

COMMUNITY CLASS PRE-TRAINING SURVEY ANSWERS

Community Class Pre-Training Survey Answers

The Gospel

1. At what point must a person get to in their lives before they can be saved?
    Answer: To a point of brokenness; they must realize they are lost without Christ.

2. What two things will a person need to act upon in order to be saved?
    A. Repentance.
    B. Ask Christ to forgive and save them.

3. What is the central theme of the gospel?
    Answer: That man is lost and God sent His Son Jesus to save man by dying the death that man deserved.

4. What does "whosoever salvation" mean to you?
    Answer: God's free gift of salvation is for every one of all nations.

5. Can children be saved?
    Answer: Yes.
    Can children die and go to hell if they were not saved during their lifetime?
    Answer: If past the age of accountability, yes they do go to hell.

Great Commission

1. Is the Great Commission for the church, the pastor, or for every believer?
    Answer: Every believer.

2. Does the Great Commission include salvation, baptism, Christian education, or just salvation? Answer: All of the above are included in the Great Commission.

3. Is the Great Commission for every generation?
   Answer: Yes.
   When did it begin?
   Answer: Following Christ's resurrection when the church began.
   When does the Great Commission end?
   Answer: When Christ returns for His church.

4. Is there urgency to the Great Commission?
   Answer: Yes.
   If yes, why?
   Answer: Lost people die every day and Christ can return at any moment.

5. What are some of the rewards and blessings that come with having a part in the Great Commission work?
   Answer: To know that God is using you to serve Him.

Devotional Life

1. Do you have a regular Bible reading schedule on a daily basis?
   Answer: Yes.

2. How would you describe your private prayer life?
   Answer: Prayer and reading the Bible.

3. Define worship?
   Answer: Outward expression or response to God for what He has done for us.

4. Would you describe your spiritual life growing, stationary, or in a reversal?
   Answer: Stationary.

5. Is your devotional life spent with a friend, spouse, or by yourself?
   Answer: Me and my spouse.

Leadership Abilities

1. Would you consider yourself to be a follower or a leader?
   Answer: A leader.

2. Do you believe leaders are born or developed?
   Answer: Some people have innate leadership abilities, while other leadership skills are learned.

3. Do you see leadership as a gift or a skill?
   Answer: Both.

4. If you had the opportunity to develop your leadership abilities would you?
   Answer: It depends on the leadership role.

5. When leadership opportunities avail themselves are you likely to take advantage of them?
   Answer: Yes, if I believed that is where the Lord wanted me to be.

Spiritual Gifts

1. What would you consider your spiritual gift to be? A teacher, prophet (preacher), or helps?
   Answer: A servant/teacher.

2. How do you think that your spiritual gift fits into the Great Commission work?
   Answer: By serving others in order to bring them under the Word of God and that they would hopefully see Christ through my actions of service.

3. Do you see your gift as a stewardship in the Great Commission work?
   Answer: Yes.

4. How do you think you should go about developing your spiritual gift?
   Answer: By studying the Bible and learning from the example of other Christians.

5. Would you like to be able to help others develop their spiritual gifts?
   Answer: Yes, in the children's ministry.

COMMUNITY CLASS POST-TRAINING SURVEY

Community Class Post-Training Survey

Lesson 1

1. How do you view the importance of the gospel after seeing the gospel work in the lives of children?

   _____

   _____

   _____

2. 2.Based on Deuteronomy 6 how have you seen the gospel work in the lives of your children?

   _____

   _____

   _____

3. How has sharing the gospel with others blessed your life?

   _____

   _____

   _____

4. In what ways has God used you in reaching children for the Lord?

   _____

   _____

   _____

Lesson 2

1. Why do you feel a personal responsibility to the Great Commission?

_____

_____

_____

2. What did you do to have victory in overcoming doubts, fears, and distractions in order to share the gospel?

_____

_____

_____

3. How has your victories in winning the lost affected other soul-winners around you?

_____

_____

_____

Lesson 3

1. After working in the children's ministry, why are you convinced that children are a priority to the kingdom of heaven?

_____

_____

_____

2. After raising your own children, why are you convinced of the importance of training children for the Lord in the home?

_____

_____

_____

Lesson 4

1. How has Scripture memory helped in your presentation of the gospel?

   _____

   _____

   _____

2. As a ministry leader how has having a planned presentation of the gospel helped?

   _____

   _____

   _____

3. After working with children and their salvation, why is it so important to give them an assurance of salvation?

   _____

   _____

   _____

Lesson 5

1. How has it helped you to memorize Scripture when presenting believers-baptism to children?

   _____

   _____

   _____

2. How have you utilized illustrations while presenting believers-baptism?

_____

_____

_____

3. What is the importance of enforcing salvation by grace alone while presenting believers-baptism?

_____

_____

_____

Lesson 6

1. Having been in the children's ministry how do you see the importance of making disciples of other faithful men?

_____

_____

_____

2. How has your leadership grown after having spent time in the children's ministry?

_____

_____

_____

3. How has the training and example of others helped you to apply ministry leadership?

_____

_____

_____

Lesson 7

1. How have you seen the importance of the local church in the children's ministry?

   _____

   _____

   _____

2. How has your service to the Lord grown while serving in the children's ministry?

   _____

   _____

   _____

3. How has your leadership grown while serving in the children's ministry?

   _____

   _____

   _____

4. How has your stewardship to the Lord grown while serving in the children's ministry?

   _____

   _____

COMMUNITY CLASS POST-TRAINING SURVEY ANSWERS

Community Class Post-Training Survey Answers

Answers:

Lesson 1

1. How do you view the importance of the gospel after seeing the gospel work in the lives of children?
    Answer: The earlier we reach them with the gospel the better it will be for them and the greater the opportunity we have to reach the parents.

2. Based on Deuteronomy 6 how have you seen the gospel work in the lives of your children?
    Answer: We have to put the Word of God in front of our children every day and be consistent.

3. How has sharing the gospel with others blessed your life?
    Answer: Sharing the gospel with others has changed my life because of seeing how it has changed other's lives for God. That blesses my life.

4. In what ways has God used you in reaching children for the Lord?
    Answer: I have watched my own children come to Christ through faithfully sharing the gospel. I have taught in Christian schools for 28 years and watched how the gospel has changed many students' lives. I have worked in the bus ministry for over 40 years and have seen the gospel change whole homes.

Lesson 2

1. Why do you feel a personal responsibility to the Great Commission? Answer: Because Jesus said "go" to all the world and preach the gospel and that includes everyone, including me.

2. What did you do to have victory in overcoming doubts, fears, and distractions in order to give out the gospel?
Answer: I focused on the Word of God and prayed to the living God.

3. How has your victories in winning the lost affected other soul-winners around you?
Answer: I lead by example and they see and desire to follow my example.

Lesson 3

1. After working in the children's ministry, why are you convinced that children are a priority to the kingdom of heaven?
Answer: It became obvious that children must be reached while they are young and open to the Lord's call.

2. After raising your own children, why are you convinced of the importance of training children for the Lord in the home?
Answer: The children spend the most time in the home, and we can point them in the Lord's direction.

Lesson 4

1. How has Scripture memory helped in your presentation of the gospel?
   Answer: I do not have to fumble around with pages in the Bible to quote Scripture. I can be easily prompted by the Holy Spirit of what Scripture to use.

2. As a ministry leader how has it helped to have a planned presentation of the gospel?
   Answer: The planned presentation keeps me on task.

3. After working with children and their salvation why is it so important to give them an assurance of salvation?
   Answer: The doubts will show up as soon as you finish giving the gospel to the child.

Lesson 5

1. How has it helped you to memorize Scripture when presenting believers-baptism to children?
   Answer: It helps me to present baptism as soon as the profession of faith is made.

2. How have you utilized illustrations while presenting believers-baptism?
   Answer: I use my hands to picture Jesus' death, burial, and resurrection in presenting baptism.

3. What is the importance of enforcing salvation by grace alone when presenting believers-baptism?

Answer: Baptism is obedience to show that you have been saved, which takes place after salvation.

Lesson 6

1. Having been in the children's ministry, how do you see the importance of making disciples of other faithful men?
   Answer: Most men get married and have children and their children need a dad to disciple them. Without reaching the dads discipleship is much less likely to happen.

2. How has your leadership grown after having spent time in the children's ministry?
   Answer: My convictions have grown and that has motivated me to do what I can do to reach the next generation for Christ.

3. How has the training and example of others helped you to apply ministry leadership?
   Answer: I watched the good examples of men and decided to follow their leadership.

Lesson 7

1. How have you seen the importance of the local church in the children's ministry?
   Answer: The church is their eternal family when their earthly family is gone.

2. How has your service to the Lord grown while serving in the children's ministry?

Answer: The children's ministry gives me the opportunity to exercise my God given gifts and to grow in grace and knowledge.

3. How has your leadership grown while serving in the children's ministry?

   Answer: The concern for the future generation of children grows while working with the current generation of children.

4. How has your stewardship to the Lord grown while serving in the children's ministry?

   Answer: I want to spend more time in reaching children, exercising my gifts in reaching them, along with being willing to give more of my finances in reaching them.

INITIAL SELECTED BIBLIOGRAPHY

Anthony, Michael. *Perspectives on the Children's Spiritual Formation: 4 Views*. Nashville, TN: B & H Academic, 2006.

Barna, George. *Transforming Children into Spiritual Champions*. Ventura: Regal Books, 2003.

Barnes, Albert. *Barnes' Notes, The Gospels*. Grand Rapids, MI: Baker Book House, 1885.

Beckwith, Ivy. *Postmodern Children's Ministry: Ministry to Children in the 21st Century*. Grand Rapids, MI: Zondervan, 2004.

Bridges, Charles. *A Commentary on Proverbs*. Carlisle: The Banner of Truth Trust, 1846.

Christenson, Larry. *The Christian Family*. Minneapolis, MN: Bethany Fellowship, 1970.

Clarke, Adam. *Matthew to Acts*. Vol. 5 of *Clarke's Commentaries*. New York, NY: Abingdon Press, 1832.

Closson, Don. *Kids, Classrooms, & Contemporary Education.* Grand Rapids, MI: Kregel Publications, 2000.

Dawn, Marva J. *Is it a Lost Cause: Having the Heart of God for the Church's Children.* Grand Rapids, MI: William B. Eerdmans Publishing Company, 1997.

DeMoss, Nancy Leigh. *Lies Women Believe: And the Truth that Sets them Free.* Chicago, IL: Moody Publishers, 2001.

Gangel, Kenneth O. and Warren S. Benson. Christian Education: Its History and Philosophy. Chicago, IL: Moody Press, 1993.

Horton, Ronald A. *Christian Education: Its Mandate and Mission.* Greenville: Bob Jones University Press, 1992.

Jeremiah, David. *I Never Thought I'd See the Day: Culture at the Crossroads.* New York, NY: Yates & Yates Publishers, 2011.

Kent, Homer A., Jr. *The Pastoral Epistles: Studies in 1 and 2 Timothy and Titus.*Chicago, IL: Moody Press, 1982.

Kienel, Paul A. *A History of Christian School Education* (Colorado Springs, CO: Purposeful Design Publications, 2005.

Lockerbie, D. Bruce. *A Passion for Learning.* Colorado Springs, CO: Purposeful Design Publications, 2007.

Morris, Henry M. *The Genesis Record: A Scientific and Devotional Commentary on the Book of Beginnings.* San Diego, CA: Creation-Life Publications, 1976.

Parr, Steve R. *Sunday School That Really Works: A Strategy for Connecting Congregations and Communities.* Grand Rapids, MI: Zondervan, 2005.

Rainer, Thom S. *Breakout Churches.* Grand Rapids, MI: Zondervan, 2005.

Richards, Lawrence O. *Children's Ministry.* Grand Rapids, MI: Zondervan, 1983.

Spurgeon, Charles H. *Come Ye Children: Practical Help Telling Children about Jesus.* Ross-Shire: Christian Focus Publications, 2003.

The Holy Bible. King James Version.

Towns, Elmer L. *10 Sunday Schools that Dared to Change.* Ventura: Regal Books, 1993.

Walvoord, John F., and Roy B. Zuck. *The Bible Knowledge Commentary: An Exposition of the Scriptures.* Wheaton, IL: Victor Books, 1985.

Westeroff, John H., III. *Will our Children have Faith.* Harrisburg, PA: Morehouse Publishing, 2000.

Wiersbe, Warren. *The Bible Exposition Commentary, Vol. 1 of Ephesians to Revelation.* Colorado Springs, CO: Chariot Victor Publishing, 1999.

Dissertations

Kennedy, Michael. Parent – Driven Discipleship: Equipping Parents at Central Baptist Church in Americus, GA. To More Effectively Disciple their Teenagers (D.Min. Dissertation, Luther Rice University, 2008).

Seymour, Mark Benson. "A Guide to Children's Ministry" (D.Min. diss., Luther Rice University, 1988), 19.

Twigg, Harold Byron. "Train Up a Child – A Children's Church Manual" (D.Min. Diss., Luther Rice University, 1982).

Whatley, Jon Lyle. "So now You've got a Children's Church" (D.Min. diss., Luther Rice University, 1982).

Interviews

Atkenson, Chris. Interviewed by Andrew Knight, South Windsor, CT, October 27, 2011.

Burke, Erven. Interviewed by Andrew Knight, South Windsor, CT, October 27, 2011.

Crichton, Bob. Interviewed by Andrew Knight, South Windsor, CT, October 28, 2011.

Scott, Paul. Interviewed by Andrew Knight, Jacksonville, FL, October 1, 2013.

Teresa, Haney. Interviewed by Andrew Knight, Jacksonville, FL, January 2, 2014.

Journal Articles

Allison, John P., and Judy V. Allison. "Parenting as Discipleship." *Ashland Theological Journal* (1997): 53.

Barna, George. "Research Shows Parenting Approach Determines whether Children become Devoted Christians." *The Barna Group* (2009): 2.

Bunge, Marcia J. "Biblical and Theological Perspectives on Children, Parents, and 'Best Practices' for Faith Formation: Resources for Children, Youth, and Family Ministry Today." *A Journal of Theology* (Winter 2008): 349.

Freeman, Lynda. "Sizing up Sunday School Curriculum: How to Find the Perfect Fit." *Your Church* (May/June 2008): 42.

Hayes, Edward L. "Evangelism of Children." *Bibliotheca Sacra* (July 1975): 251.

Hegg, David W. "Children and Congregational Worship: When, Why, and How?" *Reformation and Revival* (Winter 2001): 109.

Kennedy, John W. "The 4-14 Window: The Push on Child Evangelism Targets the Critical Early Years." *Christianity Today* (July 2004): 53.

Lovik, Gordon H. "Christian Education." *Central Bible Quarterly* (Spring 1966): 6.

Peterson, Roger L. "Secularism in the Sunday School." Central Bible Quarterly (Winter 1978): 5.

Pettegrew, Larry D. "Biblical Principles for Children's Work." *Central Bible Quarterly* (Fall 1967): 34.

Whitehead, Daniel C. "A Successful Children's Church Program." *Central Bible Quarterly* (Winter 1973): 4.

Willimon, William H. "Preaching to Children." *Faith and Mission* 3, no. 1 (Fall 1985): 26.

Internet Sources

Barna, George. "Americans are most Worried about Children's Future." The Barna Group. http://www.barna.org/family-kids-articles/97-americans-are-most-worried-about-childrens-future (accessed October 12, 2011).

Barna, George. "Survey Reveals Challenges Faced by Young People." The Barna Group. http://www.barna.org/family-kids-articles/96-survey-reveals-challenges-faced-by-young-people (accessed October 12, 2011).

Barna, George. "Wherever My Mind Takes Me, America's Most Secular Cities."Sarvodaya. http://romneymanassa. wordpress.com/2013/04/16/americas-most-secular-and-religious-cities/ (accessed September 9, 2013).

Coleman, Jasmine. "Crowed Planet: Global Population Hits 7 Billion." The Guardian. Hhtp://www.guardian.co.uk/world/2011/oct/31/seven-billion-baby-born-Philippians; accessed November 6, 2011.

Unknown, Author. "Population of Florida 2013." World Population Review. http://worldpopulationreview.com/united-states/florida (accessed September 12, 2013).

Made in the USA
Middletown, DE
12 March 2021